exl175
R.

A guide to the Cleveland Way

Books by Richard Sale

A guide to the Cotswold Way (1980)
A visitor's guide to the Cotswolds (1982)
A walker's guide to Europe (1983) with Arthur Howcroft
A Cambrian Way (1983)
The Wye Valley (1984)
Dorset (1985) with Tom Ang
Owain Glyndwr's Way (1985)
The ancient ways of Lakeland (1986) with Arthur Lees

Richard Sale

A GUIDE TO
The Cleveland Way

Constable · London

First published in Great Britain 1987
by Constable & Company Ltd
10 Orange Street London WC2H 7EG
Copyright © 1987 by Richard Sale
ISBN 0 09 467220 2
Set in Palatino 9pt by
Inforum Ltd, Portsmouth
Printed and bound in Great Britain
by the Bath Press, Avon

Contents

Acknowledgements

I would like to thank those people who assisted me both on and off the Way, but especially the staff of the York City Library, whose assistance was invaluable.

I thank Susan Shorland for having assisted with the mapping, and Mike Rogers who was largely responsible for the Appendix on the geology of the Way.

I thank Sally, Bob and Martin of Bristol and West Photography for all their help.

All photographs in this book were taken with Pentax cameras and equipment.

R.S.
1986

Illustrations

Maps

Plans

Preface

Under the provisions of the National Parks and Access to the Countryside Act of 1949, the ability to create new rights of way to allow the setting–up of continuous long–distance footpaths became law. The government agencies operating the new system did not, however, rush ahead to create a network of such paths, preferring a more cautious approach in the hope of taking the bodies representing country interests, landowners etc. with them, rather than creating confrontation at the same time.

It was not for many years, as a result, that the first official long–distance footpath came into existence, with the opening of the Pennine Way in 1965. It was entirely appropriate that the Pennine Way should be the first route, a footpath traversing the backbone of England and finishing in Scottish border country, and a way pioneered by Tom Stephenson who had campaigned so thoughtfully and for so long to bring it into existence.

The Pennine Way took a line across the highest land in the old county of Yorkshire, traversing also the Yorkshire Dales National Park. But Yorkshire was a big county, and there were 2 other areas of high land within it of such scenic delight that they attracted the attention of route planners.

One of these areas was the North York Moors, and its coastal edge, made into one of Britain's National Parks by the 1949 Act. Work on a route started as early as 1953, and it soon became obvious that the coastal section of the Way was most easily produced by following Cleveland Street, a Roman road that linked the coastal signal stations from Saltburn to Scarborough. To visit a representative selection of Moors scenery, and to sample some of the best of the views, the plateau walking took in the Hambleton and Cleveland Hills. The Cleveland Plain section around Guisborough posed problems, with its concentration of industrial waste sites and farmland, but these were overcome, and at a ceremony at Helmsley — centre for the National Park Information Service — on 24 May 1969, Britain's second official long–distance path was opened.

The finally agreed route follows the Hambleton Hills from Helmsley to Osmotherley, and the Cleveland Hills from there to Guisborough. It crosses a short section of the Cleveland Plain to reach the North Sea at Saltburn, from where it closely follows Cleveland Street to Scarborough. From there a further seven miles of clifftop walking completes the 100–mile Cleveland Way at Filey. From Filey the newer Wolds Way traverses the third of Yorkshire's upland areas to reach the Humber, and another official route, the Viking Way.

Throughout its length the Cleveland Way is well waymarked, more frequently with the Countryside Commission's official 'badge', a white acorn, but occasionally with the older, very attractive wooden signposts which have been reduced in number by coastal erosion, the elements and, sadly, by vandalism and souvenir hunters. In one section, where the route follows the line of the Lyke Wake Walk, waymarking is supplemented by the disc–markers of that footpath.

The route rises to only about 1500 feet which, in comparison to England's highest peaks, seems relatively low. Do not be deceived. As the notes on the area's weather in the section on the Moors indicates, the route is exposed and can experience sudden weather changes. It is imperative that the Wayfarer be prepared for the unexpected.

That said, the route is without doubt worthwhile, offering in its short length the greatest contrast in scenery of any of Britain's long–distance footpaths, and some of the finest walking in all its scenic categories.

A note on mapping

Within the book strip maps are given at an approximate scale of 1:25,000, using conventional map symbols.

However, these maps are not definitive, being intended as a guide, and walkers are advised to carry their own Ordnance Survey maps.

The whole route, apart from the section from Scarborough to Filey, is covered by the two double–sided, 1:25,000, Outdoor Leisure maps, Nos 26 and 27. With these two the walker has little need for anything else, as the final section of the route is a straightforward clifftop walk. Should he wish to cover that at the same scale, however, he must obtain TA 08/09/18 (No 624)

The North York Moors National Park is also covered by the older 1 inch to 1 mile Tourist Map (Map No 2 of the series). The Cleveland Way leaves this map for two sections, between Skelton and Skinningrove, and, again, from Scarborough to Filey.

The Landranger series of maps, at 1:50,000, has not been kind to the Cleveland Way, five being required to cover the route. Though it seems unlikely that anyone should want to purchase all these just to follow the Way, they are listed below:

  100 Malton and Pickering
   99 Northallerton and Ripon
   93 Middlesbrough and Darlington
   94 Whitby
  101 Scarborough

The Country Code

Enjoy the countryside and respect its life and work
Guard against all risk of fire
Fasten all gates
Keep dogs under close control
Keep to public paths across farmland
Use gates and stiles to cross field boundaries
Leave all livestock, machinery and crops alone
Take your litter home
Help to keep all water clean
Protect wildlife, plants and trees
Make no unnecessary noise

The North York Moors

The old county of Yorkshire covered 3,923,359 acres, making it the largest county in England by a huge margin. It was, in fact, over 10 per cent of England's total land area. The county was divided into three Ridings, the word deriving from the Norse 'ridden', a division. It is usually contended that the word meant one–third, explaining the lack of a South Riding, but there is not universal acceptance for so tight a definition.

The North Riding, within which all except the last couple of miles of the Cleveland Way was confined, comprised 1,354,664 acres, a very good approximation to one–third of the whole. The county boundary re–organisation of the early 1970s swept away the old Yorkshire, distributing the North Riding between the new counties of North Yorkshire and Cleveland. While this had the marginal advantage of giving additional status to the ancient name Cleveland, it removed one of the great geographical and political divisions of England. For the purpose of this particular chapter, the new allocation of land will be ignored. If the old boundaries are good enough for the county cricket club, who am I to argue?

Yorkshire's East Riding comprised the chalk wolds which reach the sea as the chalky white cliffs of Flamborough Head just south of our terminal town of Filey, and the Holderness Plain, a fertile boulder clay area squashed between the wolds and the sea. The West Riding had the Pennines, England's greatest hill range and including Mickle Fell, Yorkshire's highest peak, running the length of the old western boundary with Derbyshire, Lancashire and Westmoreland. To the east of the Pennines is the Vale of York — or Mowbray as it is locally known — through which ran the border between the West and North Ridings. The North Riding includes the high plateau of the North York Moors, bounded on three sides by the Vales of Pickering and York and the Cleveland Plain, and on the fourth side by the North Sea.

Cleveland is said to have derived its name from the cliffs that faced the Danish invaders when they came across the sea to the North Riding, but it is equally possible that the name is from the

Saxon 'cleave', clay, which is an absolutely accurate description
of the Plain's soil, boulder clay laid down by the Ice Age glaciers.
The Cleveland Wayfarer is often aware of the cleave, filling up
the tread of his boots.

The Moors that lie south of the Cleveland Plain are one of
Britain's 10 National Parks, the Park taking as its symbol Ralph
Cross, one of the many moorland crosses. The Moors are not
high, in a relative sense, not reaching the 1500–foot contour at the
highest point — crossed by the Way — but form a compact mass
sufficiently high and extensive to create its own weather, and to
have a profound influence on the county. It is estimated that the
Moors regulate 10 per cent of Yorkshire's water and that the
water loss when 6000 acres of moorland were seriously damaged
by fire in 1976 would have supplied Middlesbrough for several
weeks.

The geology of the Moors, and the coast and vales that form its
boundaries, is dealt with in Appendix I. Geographically the
moors form a high plateau, with a distinct ridge running east–
west that forms the watershed. In consequence the rivers drain
north to Cleveland, and south to the Vale of Pickering, and such
roads that approach the plateau also follow this north–south
pattern. The most distinctive valley is that of Bilsdale which
almost splits the plateau, and divides the softer, greener
Hambleton Hills from the rest of the moorland mass. Not that
Bilsdale is the reason for the difference in vegetation between the
western area of the plateau and its centre. The Hambletons are
limestone–based, the rock giving us the cliffs above Gormire as
well as a greater variety of plant life, but as Black Hambleton is
approached the soil quality, and therefore plant variety, declines.
The limestone cliffs, and the land above them, support a
wonderful richness of vegetation, though some of the original
varieties have been removed by indiscriminate collecting. In the
wooded vales around Helmsley there is another fine range of
species, including orchids, but the habitats are far from secure.

The central plateau is definitive moorland: land stripped of its
woodland cover and, therefore, of any chance of replacing soil
nutrients. The lack of nutrients produces a reduced vegetation
cover and less resistance to the leaching action of rain which
further impoverishes the soil. What is produced is a thin, acidic

soil; in places where the water drainage is poor, an acid peat is built up, the same peat that holds, sponge–like, Cleveland's water. The peat beds do allow a slight variation in plant life, but in the main the Moors support only heather: it has been estimated that one square mile produces, each year, 3000 million flowers. The ling is home for grouse, but is a much more hostile environment for animals in general than was the woodland it replaced. Someone once suggested that had those in power in 1815 known of the North York Moors, there would have been no need to send Napoleon to St. Helena.

On the coast, as the Moors end, either dramatically with a tumble over high cliffs or in a gentler downsweep, the soil becomes richer, with its covering of boulder clay, and plant life increases, both in variety and abundance. The area has a reputation, not wholly deserved, for being cold and wet, and generally miserable. In reality the Moors are not wet at all, the prevailing wind placing them in the rain shadow of the Pennines, producing an annual rainfall only about 20 per cent of that of the Lake District or of Snowdonia, both of which lie on the western coast. A comparison of statistics shows that the Moor's rainfall is comparable to that of Cornwall, while the coastal section of our walk — being in the rain shadow of the Moors — is even drier, comparable to Kent. Frequently Whitby and Scarborough stand beside Torquay in tables of sunshine hours

It would be wrong, however, to suggest that the Moors are entirely equable, or that equally favourable comparisons could be made in winter. The western escarpment of the Moors' plateau, the Hambleton Hills, presents a solid face to the prevailing winds from across the Vale of York. The wind is deflected upwards to the delight of the glider pilot, above Sutton Bank and along the scarp face, to be channelled towards the plateau. This gives the correct impression that the wind really does blow across the Moors with a greater strength. If that wind is cold, increasing loss of body heat because of the now famous wind chill factor, and if there is some water in it to further increase the walker's heat loss, then the continuous lack of shelter can turn an invigorating sea–level breeze into a raw, biting wind in a very short time.

In winter the westerly and south-westerly winds depart, to be replaced by a wind from the north or north-east, with nothing between it and the Arctic. When this wind blows the Moors become a really inhospitable place, and it is television pictures of snow–covered moor and road from mid–winter which colour people's vision of the area. Occasionally this polar wind can arrive unexpectedly in May or June, and as it rises over the Moors it can bring completely unexpected falls in temperature accompanied by a sudden shower either of icy rain or of sleet. While this variety adds to the joy of living in England, one of the few countries where it is possible to experience all four seasons in the space of just one day, it can ruin a pleasant walk. So, be prepared for the worst even if the day seems set fair.

Another very local effect, one usually limited to the coastal section of the walk, although it is seen further inland, is the 'fret' or 'roak', the North Sea mist. This occurs when the prevailing warm westerlies rise above an on–shore–moving band of colder, wetter air. The fog formed is cold and damp and can be quite extensive. The usual advice to tourists is to move inland and upwards, but that is little consolation to a walker on the coastal path.

The first men to settle the area would have had few of these problems, if men lived in Yorkshire at the same time as the animals whose bones have been found in Kirkdale Cave, about 6 miles east of the start of the Way. Those animals were hyena, lion and rhinoceros, animals associated with a much warmer climate. With the coming of the Ice Age, any men who did live here would have been driven south, to return only about 8000 years ago as the ice retreated northward.

Those who came to Yorkshire in the wake of the ice were Mesolithic hunters, evidence of their occupation of the area being the pygmy flints still to be found near Sneck Yate, on Whorlton and Carlton Moors, and near Burton Howe. We have to wait several thousand years for the arrival of Neolithic man, however, before there exists on the Moors a culture with remains discernible to the tourist as opposed to the specialist. In one sense the very existence of the Moors themselves is a reminder of Neolithic man: it was he who heralded the agrarian revolution, and came in search of easily cleared ground to farm and trees to fell for fuel and shelter. The hilltops had a sandier, more easily worked soil and sparser tree covering, making clearance easier. The local rock was too soft for tools, so these were imported from the Lakeland axe factories at Langdale. Unfortunately, once cleared of tree cover, the rain leached the limited nutrients from the soil, the farmer moved on to clearings new, and the heather filled in behind him.

The other, tangible, reminder of Neolithic man is his burial chamber, the long barrow. In other parts of the country these are numerous, but here they are few — the land was not that hospitable — but one does lie on the route, above Kepwick. When the Bronze Age culture superceded the Neolithic, the local climate had improved, making the Moors more acceptable as a permanent home, and as a consequence there is a large number of round barrows on the high tops. The Way goes close to several well–known sites where the barrows are clustered, cemetery–like — for instance Drake Howe on Cringle Moor and Burton Howe beyond the Way's high point on Urra Moor. Round barrows are associated with an influx of Beaker Folk, so–called from a distinctive pottery vessel usually associated with Stonehenge, though the searcher for stone circles on the Moors will be disappointed. They probably did exist, but what is left is very poorly preserved, and none lies very close to the Way.

It is to the Bronze Age that many of the small cairns that litter the Moors are allocated, though it is not clear precisely what they are. It is assumed that they are funereal in some way, either marking the spot of cremations or a processional way, but insufficient work has been carried out on them.

As the Bronze Age became the Iron Age, the climate of Yorkshire became colder and wetter, driving the new invaders, now more usually known by the blanket term Celt, down into the valleys. One feature of the new age is well represented on the route, however — the hill fort. These may have been used in a purely defensive way, strongholds into which the local farmers retreated when danger threatened, though some of the larger ones, for instance the huge Maiden Castle in Dorset, were permanently settled. The Cleveland Way passes two sites, at Roulston Scar and Boltby Scar, each of which is of a type known as promontory. At each a spur of moorland exists, offering adequate natural defence from the scarp slope on two sides of a triangle. On the third side, the moorland connection, a defensive ditch has been dug, a rampart raised.

It was, perhaps, to these forts that the Celts, a local tribe called the Brigantes, fell back when the area was occupied by the Romans in the wake of the invasion of AD 43. The Brigantian Queen, Cartimandua, was pro–Roman, to such an extent that she handed over to them Caratacus, who had led the Celts in Wales in their resistance to Rome. Unwisely, however, she then divorced her husband, Venutius, in favour of his armour–bearer, a move that led to civil war, with Cartimandua fleeing to the Romans. The Romans had used the Brigantes as a buffer between themselves and the Picts of Scotland, and fear of a hostile alliance between these war–like tribes led them to swift action. Venutius had started to fortify the area around Stanwick, north of Richmond, with ditches and ramparts, but the work was not completed, a Roman army under Petitius Ceralis making very sure of that.

The Romans were not interested in the cold, wet Moors, and Roman remains are few, although, of course, they abound in the lowland valleys of Yorkshire: York — Eboracum — was a major centre in Roman Britain. Exceptions to this rule are the string of signal stations erected along the coast, many of which lie on or near the Way. The stations are almost certainly not contemporary with the final defeat of the Brigantes but date from the fourth century, when sea–borne Anglian invaders were tormenting the Romanised inhabitants of north–east England. By then the Romans had trouble at home, and were unable to offer more than token support to this far–flung corner of the Empire. One day the stations signalled that the pirates were coming again, but there was no one to receive the signal. The signallers were killed, their stations wasted.

The invading Angles initially founded two kingdoms, Deira including the area of the Moors, and Bernicia to the north, though these were combined, by conquest, into Northumbria under the kingship of Edwin. Edwin was pagan but he married Ethelburga, a Christian from Saxon Kent. Bede tells of Edwin's conversion, a conversion induced by a foiled assassination and the survival of his queen and child during a difficult labour. The assassination was prevented by Lilla, one of Edwin's ministers, at the cost of his own life. Lilla was buried with great reverence, and some gold, in a Bronze Age barrow now called Lilla Howe. But though Edwin was converted, in as much as his new child was baptised, he hesitated to have himself baptised. First he wanted the new god to grant him victory over his enemies, a request which, considering that pagan kings were often deified, does not seem unreasonable, even if it does seem blasphemous. Edwin was granted(?) his victory, becoming king of a greater part of England, though not of his father-in-law's Kentish kingdom, and was baptised on Easter Day AD 627 in the first, and hastily built, York Minster.

When Edwin died in battle in 632, Northumbria hovered on the brink of a return to paganism, but King (and Saint) Oswald with the help of his great friend St. Aidan, the founder of Lindisfarne monastery, made Christianity the official religion. Some time after Oswald's death, in about 656, abbeys were founded at Whitby and at Lastingham, now within the boundaries of the Moors' National Park. Following its founding, Whitby was home for England's first poet, Caedmon; a further first can be seen at Kirkdale Church — though this is not on the route — where a sundial bears the earliest known English inscription.

The Angles gave us the suffixes '-ley', '-ton' and '-ham', referring to settlements or woodland clearings, which crop up so frequently throughout this area. Two centuries after its founding, Whitby Abbey was plundered by new North Sea-borne invaders, the Danes, who changed the nature of the place naming by using '-by' to signify settlement. Recently, with the excavation and exciting reconstruction of Viking York, that city has become the centre for study of these new invaders of the north-east. That is appropriate because York was the capital of a kingdom that, more or less, corresponded to modern Yorkshire, a Danish kingdom that survived until the murder of the ruthless pagan Eric Bloodaxe, in the mid–tenth century. Some of the finest Danish relics in the area, grave slabs, are also at St. Gregory's, Kirkdale.

It is probably to the Danes that we also owe the moorland

crosses that are such a feature of the National Park, many of them named for individuals no longer remembered. Frequently the crosses have been broken off and, as with many such instances throughout Britain, these are called Stump's Cross. One was reputedly named for a Danish soldier who lost both legs, hacked off in a moorland battle, but who fought on, on his stumps!

The history of Danish invasion and, to an extent, of Danish England, is one of raid and battle. It is therefore a surprise to discover that the Danes and Angles lived, at peasant–farmer level, in relative harmony, sharing village sites or having sites on opposite sides of a river. In each case the peasants wanted water, a river ford, shelter and reasonable land. If well treated they probably just got on with life, noticing the petty squabbles of their lords only when directly called into an army or when a different man arrived to collect the taxes.

The coming of Tostig would therefore have been noticed. He had been put in charge of northern lands by his brother, King Harold Godwinson, when the latter succeeded to the crown of England. Harold and Tostig were half–Danish: following Eric Bloodaxe's death, England had been controlled by English kings of Danish descent rather than by Danes; and when Harold banished his brother for misuse of power it was to Norway that Tostig fled. He returned with Harold Hardrada and an army, bent on vengeance, though he found only death, at Stamford Bridge, near York.

But even as Harold was celebrating his victory, news came that a new and even more potent enemy had landed near Hastings. The Normans had come.

The Anglo–Danish Archbishop of York, Aldred, crowned William at Westminster, but the North was a long way from London, and rebellions against the newcomers were frequent. In 1069 York was captured, with the loss of several thousand Normans. This time William had had enough, and he marched with an army to 'harry the North'. Stories were later told of the devastation, bodies rotting in the fields for want of people to bury them. Certainly the Domesday survey notes frequently that villages, and even towns, were 'waste'.

In Yorkshire, even more than elsewhere except, perhaps, in the frontier country of Wales, the Norman lords needed castles to protect their persons. The Cleveland Way starts near one such castle, Helmsley, and finishes not far removed from another at Scarborough. In time the Normans became acceptably English, but then the North Riding lived through an uncomfortable couple of centuries as frontier land between their king and the war–like Scots. The Battle of the Standard, when the army of King Stephen defeated the Scots under King David, was fought in 1138 not far from Northallerton, to the west of the Way; and the Battle of Byland, in 1322, when the Scots defeated Edward II, involved soldiers marching along the line of the Way itself. It was during this time that the great monastic houses of Yorkshire were endowed, yielding for us the great ruins of Fountains and, on our route, of Rievaulx and Whitby, and for the peasants the start of industrialisation and a gradual improvement in their lot.

It has been said that the history of York is the history of England. Never more was that the case than during the Wars of the Roses in the third quarter of the fifteenth century. Through 30 years and many battles, St. Albans, Northampton, St. Albans again, Tewksbury and Bosworth outside our area, Wakefield and Towton within it — and the list is not exhaustive — the Lancastrian Red Rose and leaders called Henry fought the Yorkist White Rose and leaders called Edward or Richard. The Wars started with Henry IV reigning and finished with the final defeat and death of the horseless Richard III at Bosworth Field in 1485, and Henry Tudor being enthroned as Henry VII, bringing a period of peace and unparalleled prosperity to England or, at least, to the English nobility. The only sour note was Henry VIII's Dissolution of the Monasteries, which drew a characteristically belligerent response from the men of the North. The Pilgrimage of Grace started in Lincolnshire in 1536 but spread quickly to Yorkshire, where an army was formed under Robert Aske that took the castle of Pontefract and the city of Hull, and marched on Doncaster. The rising was put down and Aske executed. The area rose again in 1569 in support of Catholicism. That rebellion too was put down with many executions, but militant Catholicism rumbled on in the county. In 1605 Guy Fawkes, another Yorkshireman, was executed for his part in a real, or well–

imagined, Catholic plot to overthrow Parliament and the king. From that point on, however, there were no more religious insurrections in the county.

In 1639 Charles I came to York to demand from his loyal Yorkshiremen the money he needed to mount a campaign against the Scots, who were objecting to attempts to make them use the English prayer book. The Yorkshire nobility declined to supply the cash and Charles summoned the Long Parliament, which also defied him. On 22 August 1642 the king raised his standard at Nottingham, and the standard promptly fell over, a bad omen with which to start the Civil War. By 1644 the Parliamentarians under Lord Fairfax and his son, Sir Thomas, were, with Scottish help, besieging the Royalists, under the Earl of Newcastle, in York. A relief army under Prince Rupert crossed the Pennines and met the re–deployed Parliament army at Marston Moor. On the Parliament side was a deputy commander whose brilliance that day resulted in a crushing defeat for the Royalists, a defeat from which they never really recovered. His name was Oliver Cromwell.

Following the battle, York fell and Sir Thomas Fairfax, himself a Yorkshireman, cleared up resistance throughout the county. In recognition of Yorkshire's mighty presence in the land, 15 of the judges who tried King Charles were Yorkshiremen, and the Parliaments of 1654 and 1656 did much to soothe the grievances of the county's previously unrepresented landowners. But it was Fairfax who was sent to Holland to speak with the new king-to-be when the county grew tired of the Protectorate.

While the tides of political fortune ebbed and flowed around it, the high plateau of the Moors and its quiet dales remained much as they had always been, a place for hardy farmers persuading a precarious living from a hostile countryside. On our route we shall see no evidence of the Wars of the Roses, although we will visit places visited also by Civil Warring factions. But we will see considerable evidence of the part that the plateau, or rather, the minerals that lie beneath its surface, played in the later industrialisation of the Cleveland Plain: the Way passes the remains of the alum mines that first brought industry to the area, and also relics of the ironstone mines that laid the foundations for the development of Teeside.

It is not the North Riding, however, but the West Riding that is considered, along with Lancashire, to be the heartland of the Industrial Revolution. It was there that the major coal resources were discovered, laying the foundation for steam- and, therefore, machine-power.

Edmund Cartwright's power loom was first used in Doncaster in 1787. The effect of the steam mills was, at first, to put handworkers of the textile industries out of work. In the longer term it actually raised employment levels, but at the expense of a way of life. Steam–power was concentrated in the owner's mill, with a consequent destruction of the cottage industry in favour of compacted work forces. The villages, or the scattered homesteads, were replaced by the back-to-back terraces that still form the basis of the Northern myth popular in the south of England.

To explode that myth — though, as with all good prejudices, it is not based solely on reality — it is only necessary to visit the North York Moors or, better, to walk the Cleveland Way.

The Cleveland Way

Helmsley

It seems appropriate that a long–distance footpath that is largely
confined within the borders of the North York Moors National
Park should start in the headquarters town of the Park
Committee and Information Service. The headquarters are
situated in the Old Vicarage in Bondgate, just a short distance
from the town square.

During a restoration of All Saints Church in 1868, three square
stones with square holes in them were found and interpreted as
foundation stones for posts supporting a Saxon wattle church.
These, together with the imagined knowledge that in the seventh
century St. Aidan had preached at 'Hamlake', led the locally
famous Revd Charles Norris Gray, who served All Saints from
1870 to 1913, to suggest that there could have been a church here
from AD 200. In fact there is scant evidence for the existence of
any church long before the compilation of the Domesday Book,
and not much more for the existence of a village. The name
Helmsley derives from Helm's Clearing, suggesting that a farm
existed in the Anglo–Saxon period following the Roman
occupation of the area.

There are no Roman remains in Helmsley, although a couple of
miles to the east, near Beadlam Grange, the remains of a villa,
including a fine mosaic pavement, have been unearthed and
dated to the fourth century.

The Domesday Book describes late Saxon Helmsley. It had 13
families, two priests and a wooden church, and a total of 11½
carucates of arable land. A carucate of land was an area that could
be ploughed by an eight–ox team in one year and, as such, was
capable of a fair degree of variation. It could, perhaps, be as small
as 120 acres, though it is more usually thought to imply 160 to 180
acres. Whichever it was in the case of Helmsley, or Elmeslac as
the Norman conquerors first termed it, it hardly represented a

Feversham Memorial, Helmsley

substantial village. William I granted the lands to Robert de
Mortain, his half–brother, but when Robert rebelled against
William Rufus in 1088 the lands were confiscated and eventually
passed into the hands of Walter l'Espec.

L'Espec was Lord of Helmsley from 1120 until 1154 and during
his time the village expanded rapidly, to achieve lasting
importance and to reach the pages of recorded history: Theodoric
is recorded as priest of a church granted to the Augustinian
Canons of Kirkham; Rievaulx Abbey was founded and the first
castle at Helmsley was raised. But why did l'Espec choose to
build a castle at Helmsley and, as a consequence, increase the
village's importance and taxes? There is no simple answer to this
question, but the root cause almost certainly lies in 1138 and the
Battle of the Standard against the Scots a dozen miles to the west
of the village. All over England the Norman lords were building
castles to protect themselves from local uprisings, and in the
border countries from incursions from still-to-be-subdued Wales
and Scotland. L'Espec would have recognised that the North
York Moors offered any invading Scottish army a back door into
the Vale of York, and would have wanted to protect his lands
from attack.

A look at a relief map of the Moors shows that the high plateau
is split in only two places. One is to the east, where Newton Dale
cuts back towards Goathland Moor and the Upper Esk Valley
leads down to Grosmont, a route later taken by the Moors
Railway; the other is to the west, where Bilsdale parts the
Hambleton Hills from the main plateau, and is now followed by
the B1257 down to the Vale of Cleveland. At the mouth of the first
breach is Pickering, with a Norman castle, and at the mouth of
second is Helmsley: in addition to the strategic importance of the
village there was also, just to the south–west, beside the River
Rye, a ridge of rock offering both a solid base and an elevated
position for any defensive building.

It was not Walter l'Espec's castle that was capable of 'inspiring
feelings of astonishment and sentiments of respect in every
reflective mind, when these ruins are beheld' in an early
nineteenth–century writer. The oldest of what remains on the
ridge above Helmsley are the ruins of a castle constructed by

The West Range of Helmsley Castle

Robert de Roos, brother–in–law to l'Espec, who succeeded to the
Lordship of Helmsley when the latter died childless. And what a
castle de Roos has bequeathed us. In total it measures some 250
by 150 yards, a vast and complex array of ditches, ramparts and
stonework.

First there is an outer ditch, roughly square and extended at the
northern and southern corners (the castle is orientated, as with
the underlying rock ridge, north–west to south–east). These

extensions suggest an original, or originally intended, outer bailey which, if it had been included, would have made the castle site absolutely huge for its period.

A rampart, probably originally topped by a wooden palisade, separates this outer ditch from an inner one which is still deep enough and steep enough to be a recognisably impressive barrier, even though, as Dorothy Wordsworth so delightfully put it, the ditches have 'grown up into soft green cradles'. On top of the inner rampart of this inner ditch is a curtain wall that would probably have been as much as 15 feet high. At three of its four corners there are round turrets, the fourth corner, to the south–east, being a defended gateway. A second entrance between two round towers existed through the north–west wall, a better defended gate, though each had a drawbridge and portcullis.

About half–way along the south–east wall is the keep, always the centrepiece of a Norman castle, the last fortified refuge in times of attack. The Helmsley keep is no exception: its walls are 8 feet thick. It is, however, of very unusual design, D-shaped rather than square or rectangular. No very satisfactory explanation for this break with tradition exists. It has been suggested that the position of the keep, in the curtain wall, and therefore over the inner ditch, meant that a conventionally shaped keep could have been more easily undermined, but in view of the massive outer defences that does not seem very likely. And if the builders were so concerned about the possibility, why did they choose to put the keep there at all?

About 50 years after the first construction, the south–east gateway was further strengthened by the building of a barbican on the berm, or rampart, between the two ditches. It is through this new defensive work that the visitor, turning left at the pay booth, enters the castle, and an impressive structure it still is, despite the whole site's use as a quarry since the Civil War. The barbican consisted of a gateway with two sidewalls ending in half–round towers, these towers linked by narrow walkway walls across the inner ditch to the main curtain walls. Later still the barbican was altered — the newer brown sandstone is obvious against the older white limestone — to offer some basic accommodation to the outer garrison. The new amenities included a garderobe in the gateway's eastern tower. This word is not a genteel alternative to lavatory, but is the original word. A Norman castle's toilet facilities were basic: a hole down through the thick castle wall, discharging into the sea at coastal sites, into the moat, or just into the bottom of the wall. The stink from such an orifice was probably indescribable and is certainly best left undescribed, but the rising vapours were thought to keep moths out of clothes, so these were hung over the hole, hence — garderobe. I cannot speak for the moths, but they would certainly have kept me at bay. The subject does offer an interesting sidelight on medieval castle–dwelling, however; life was certainly not all fun in a draughty, badly sanitised castle, especially if you were the boy sent down occasionally to rake out the bottom of the garderobe chimney. One medieval castle, at least, was taken during a Crusade by sending a slim soldier to crawl up the garderobe chimney and lower the drawbridge, an episode of which it is probably best left to the reader to consider the risks!

The final building phases of Helmsley were the construction of a chapel beside the keep, though this was not used as such for very long, as its existence meant a loss of revenue to the Canons who held the local church; and of the domestic buildings on the inner south–west curtain wall. Of these only foundations remain of the Great Hall and its associated kitchen area, but the west tower, part of which is as old as the keep, and the two–storeyed buildings beside it, are much more complete, indeed the building range still has the slated roof and some original glass.

The Civil War was the only occasion on which the castle saw active service. It had been briefly besieged in 1216 by King John, kicking at the shins of Robert de Roos, a co–signatory of Magna Carta, and even more briefly by the Scots in 1322 when they looted and burned Helmsley. But it had never been truly attacked, until 1544. By then it was owned by the Duke of Buckingham and held for the king by Sir Jordan Crossland against the army of Sir Thomas Fairfax, fresh from taking York for the Parliamentarians. Despite cannon, a weapon it had never been built to withstand, the castle held out, only surrendering after three months when a relief column was defeated. The defenders were allowed to leave with honour, dignity and

'without aine molestacion', and Cromwell gave the castle to
Fairfax. Thirteen years later Buckingham's son married Fairfax's
daughter! But the castle they inherited was much changed.
Anxious to prevent its further use as a war–base, of which it was
still a very fine example, the castle was slighted, gunpowder
starting the job, the locals' desire for stone finishing it.

Buckingham was a spendthrift and he died bankrupt, his
estate, including the castle, being sold to Sir Charles Duncombe,
a London banker, whose family lived in it until they had
constructed the magnificent Duncombe Park, with the house by
Vanbrugh and grounds considered by Pevsner to be 'one of the
most extensive and boldest landscaping exercises in England'.

The arrival of the Duncombe family coincided with a further
upturn in the fortunes of Helmsley, a village which had, in any
case, been very prosperous due to the Lord's castle and nearby
Rievaulx Abbey. The Abbey had grown wealthy from sheep
farming, with Helmsley a centre for weaving, and after the
Dissolution this expertise had been transferred to work on locally
grown flax. Throughout the eighteenth century the industry
grew, and by the early nineteenth century there were over 100
looms working flax now largely brought in from Hull by
packhorse. It was not to last. The Helmsley industry was cottage–
based, and when the power looms arrived in Manchester the
local weavers rapidly become uneconomic. Many left and the
town declined: a new workhouse was built in 1851. The building
is still there in Hight Street, though it has now been converted
into pleasant flats.

But Helmsley's position, at the base of the Moors' plateau and
at the mouth of Bilsdale, meant that the late-nineteenth-century
transport boom was bound to improve its lot, so its decline was
not total. Today, the town is a pleasant, airy place, grouped
around its large market square.

The square is dominated by the Feversham Monument, built
for the second Lord Feversham, then Lord of the Major, around
1860. Depending upon whether your taste encompasses or rejects

Helmsley

the Victorian Gothic style, the monument is either a marvel or a monstrosity. It leaves little room for a neutral view.

The Black Swan Hotel on the west side of the square is altogether different: it is difficult to imagine anyone not falling in love with it. It is generally assumed that it was here William and Dorothy Wordsworth stayed, in 1802, when they were on their way to visit Mary Hutchinson, later William's wife, who lived near Scarborough. After the wedding all three stayed at Helmsley again and it was on that occasion that Dorothy described the castle ditches in her journal. But did they really stay in the Black Swan? Some have interpreted Dorothy's journal as implying that their inn was actually the Golden Lion, closer to the castle. But since that is now a butcher's shop, the Black Swan has a clear field in the race to capture the poet.

The hotel earns a commendation from Pevsner. It is, he says, a 'nice job' in contrast to the flanking Town Hall, a 'dull job'! And indeed it is a nice job, incorporating now the old Rectory, a fine half–timbered building that pre–dates the rest of the hotel by several centuries. The Rectory is, in fact, one of the oldest houses in Helmsley, being fifteenth century, about the same age as Thorpe's Cottage, itself now part of another hotel, the Feathers. Canon's Garth to the north of the church is, in part, older, having been built in the twelfth century for the Canons of Kirkham, but virtually rebuilt in the sixteenth century.

Our route starts in the square, not at the Feversham Monument but at the older market cross away towards the church. All Saints Church itself is passed, but do not miss the opportunity to visit it, if only to glimpse the work of one of the most extraordinary people to have lived in Helmsley, Vicar Gray. Grandson of a Bishop of Bristol and son of a Bishop of Cape Town, Gray obviously had an excellent pedigree for his position, one he embraced with a zeal that matched his large physical presence. His love for things spiritual involved the construction of five churches in neighbouring villages and in maintaining rectors in such a state of enthusiasm, or fear, that they would go through flood, blizzard or tempest to service them. One of his rectors was once noted as having preached to a plough–boy while he was ploughing. But Gray's zeal extended also to things secular. He

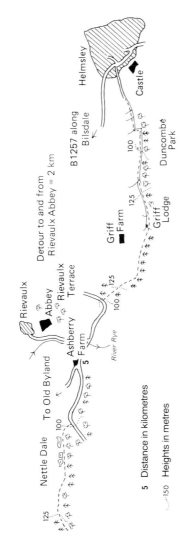

Helmsley

Castle

B1257 along
Bilsdale

Duncombe
Park

100

125

Griff
Farm

Griff
Lodge

Detour to and from
Rievaulx Abbey = 2 km

Rievaulx

Abbey

Rievaulx
Terrace

125

100

Ashberry
Farm

5

River Rye

To Old Byland

Nettle Dale

100

125

5   Distance in kilometres

150   Heights in metres

complained of housing 'utterly unfit for either man or beast', of the town drain in which 'there is enough filth to poison everybody', of the roads, of the water supply, of the postal system and of much more besides. And since he knew how, where and when to complain in order to cause maximum aggravation and was very clearly not a man to be tangled with lightly, most of his complaints resulted in corrective action.

Within All Saints Church Vicar Gray moved several monuments — causing some distress and much annoyance resulting in correspondence with the Archbishop of York from the aggrieved, but no action against the vicar — to clear walls for a series of quasi medieval murals depicting the birth of Christianity in the North of England. Here are St. Columba founding Iona, the already mentioned fictitious episode with St. Aidan, and Christian King Oswald killing the heathen British leader Cadwallon. The latter, and the knight slaughtering the dragon ('the saint of God drives Satan from Anglia') seem to personify Vicar Gray — uncompromising and utterly assured of the correctness of his ideas. The Vicar has to be admired for his social awareness and his evangelism, but his attitude towards Roman Catholicism and Methodists fell well short of anything that could be termed Christian.

Murals apart, the church has other things to offer, though the Victorian restoration involved rebuilding on a massive scale. But note the Norman door and chancel archway, the latter especially noteworthy with its outer row of grotesques; and the painted ceiling of the north aisle. Much of the woodcarving in the chancel is by Thompson of Kilburn, whose work we shall meet again. In the entrance porch the hogsback tombstone, though not particularly good of its type, is pre–Norman and as such is the oldest piece here, the only reminder of an earlier church.

Beyond All Saints the Cleveland Way goes left on a signposted lane to Rievaulx. Go to the end of this lane and over the stile into the fields beyond. Cross three fields and after the gate into the fourth, turn left down to the walled wood. The wood here, much thinned recently, is at the edge of Duncombe Park.

Follow the wood edge westward and at (595 836) after crossing two stiles, a gate to the left allows access to a wooded valley, beyond which the boundary trees of Duncombe Park are followed again. The concrete bases in the trees to the left represent all that remains of a World War Two Polish Army Camp.

At (590 834) a neat lodge is reached, a track beside which leads north to Griff Farm, in medieval times a grange of Rievaulx Abbey. We, however, go westwards with the lodge to our right, over a stile and on to a track that leads to the road at (580 841). Turn left, and pause between the canal bridge at (576 842) and the River Rye bridge at (574 843) to view the ruins of Rievaulx Abbey to the north.

Rievaulx Abbey

Rievaulx Abbey is the first of four monastic house ruins on our route. It is also the finest, complete enough to be breathtaking and yet, at the same time, sufficiently silent and ruinous to be enigmatic. The four houses — Mount Grace and Guisborough Priories and Whitby Abbey complete the quartet — were all dedicated to different monastic orders, so it is worthwhile here to consider the place of the monk in the medieval landscape, and the differences between the orders.

In the sixth century St. Benedict, born in the Central Italian province of Nursia probably in the last quarter of the fifth century, laid down specific rules for the behaviour of monks. The word 'monk' derives from the Greek 'monos', meaning single, alone, and referring at the time to the numerous hermits who lived in caves and other remote spots throughout Christian Europe. St. Benedict sought to correct the chaos of individual monks who contributed little either to the worship of God or to their locality, and also to temper the more extreme masochism practised by many of them. He gathered twelve followers on the hilltop of Monte Cassino and assumed a more apostolic life based on the principles of poverty, learning and a set daily round of prayer and worship. Whitby Abbey, the first of our quartet to be founded — or rather, re-founded — around 1100, was Benedictine.

In time the rules of St. Benedict had relaxed, and the monks had become rather well off in comparison to their peasant neighbours, since the wealth of the monasteries grew as a result of benefactions of money and land. At about the same time as the establishment of Whitby, a group of monks at Citeaux decided that things had gone too far, and that a reversion to the strict rule of St. Benedict was required. These monks were the first Cistercians. As he chronicled its foundation, the formation of the

Rievaulx Abbey from the Cleveland Way

new order is usually ascribed to Stephen Harding, an English monk who was, in fact, the second Abbot of Citeaux. The Cistercians wore only coarse wool clothing, whereas the Benedictines had linen underwear; they had only iron or wooden ornaments and vessels in their churches, whereas the Benedictines had gold; they refused tithes and rents, re-establishing the idea of a hard, independent life; and they cut back on the prayer rounds, which had become ritualised and of questionable value. They deliberately chose for their abbeys the wilder areas of the country, and their independence, which led to such things as sheep farming and local iron industries, was to have a profound effect on the economies of their regions, though they did little to enhance local learning. Rievaulx Abbey was a Cistercian monastery.

The Augustinian Canons, sometimes known as the Canons Regular or Austin Friars, founded Guisborough Priory after Whitby but before Rievaulx. The order was based on the Rule of St. Augustine, a fourth-century priest who wanted to segregate totally the temporal and secular sides of life by having priests living in a monastic order rather than among the people where they might be subjected to the agonies of worldy ambitions. In this they were very close to the Benedictines, indeed in later years, when many Benedictine monks were themselves ordained, the distinction between the orders became a little blurred.

Mount Grace Priory was founded by the Carthusian Order, the monks of which sought, at a late stage, to re-establish some of the asceticism of the original hermits. No Carthusian Priory was founded in England before the late twelfth century and there were only two before the mid-fourteenth-century expansion of the order. By the time of the foundation of Mount Grace, even the Cistercian order had been seduced by the wealth accumulated through many years of astute business. In a Carthusian house the monks lived in cells, isolated from their brethren, largely silent and spending their time in contemplation or working in their own small gardens. Their needs were attended to by lay brothers, so the monks themselves had little opportunity to become either rich or to share in any communal richness that might accrue.

Following the death of his son in a riding accident Walter l'Espec, whom we have already met at Helmsley, offered land in Ryedale to 12 Cistercian monks under William, the first Abbot. In all probability the site would not have been inspiring, sandwiched between a steep hill, the river and a tangled wood full of wolves and wild cats. A horrible and solitary place is how one contemporary visitor saw it, a sentiment shared by a traveller from a supposedly more romantic age centuries later: he saw the Abbey site in 'vast and dreadful isolation'. But Abbot William and his monks saw in the dale what they sought — seclusion, shelter and a good supply of water — and here, in 1143, they founded the Abbey in Rye Vallis, the Rye Valley. Within 35 years virtually the whole of the building had been completed, a remarkable rate of construction.

On its completion Rievaulx was the major Cistercian house in Britain, and its ruins are still considered to be among the finest monastic remains. Fountains Abbey, also in Yorkshire, was also Cistercian, as were Tintern beside the Wye, Valle Crucis and Strata Florida in Wales, and Hailes in Gloucestershire. Each was in a beautiful country setting, and none more so than Rievaulx, to reflect the Cistercian desire to be away from town life.

Of the work that dates from the earliest building phase, the largest remaining sections of Rievaulx are the nave and transepts of the church, the furthest section from the present entrance. Rievaulx was not built conventionally with the church aligned east–west, perhaps because of lack of space, but is, very roughly, on a north–south axis. It has become accepted practice to refer to the buildings as though they do have the conventional orientation and on that basis the nave is at the west end of the site. It represents the earliest large Cistercian church and is larger than any that survives in France. It is architecturally austere, in keeping with Cistercian ideals as embodied in the man who oversaw its construction, the third Abbot, St. Aelred. Aelred was a Saxon born at Hexham in 1109 who had served as a member of the household of Prince, later King, David of Scotland. When leading a mission to the Archbishop of York he heard of the Cistercians and their new Abbey, visited Rievaulx, was captivated by the simple piety of the new order, and became a

novice. He became Abbot of the Rievaulx daughter–house of
Rivesby in Lincolnshire, returned to Yorkshire as Abbot and
remained at Rievaulx until his death in 1167. Aelred was a great
monastic scholar and wrote of the Cistercians: 'our food is scanty,
our garments rough, our drink is from the stream. . . . There is
no moment for idleness or dissipation. . . . Everywhere peace,
everywhere serenity, and a marvellous freedom from the tumult
of the world.' In old age Aelred was crippled with arthritis, a
condition not assisted by the cold and damp of the monastery
where fires were viewed as an indulgence. The monks sought a
special dispensation from Citeaux to allow Aelred to sleep in the
infirmary where there was a fire, but though this was granted the
old Abbot declined, and remained in his unheated lodgings.

St. Aelred would not have approved of the major extension of
the church, to the east, that was carried out in the late twelfth
century. The extension, by the addition of quire and presbytery,
is thought to be one of the most beautiful examples of the English
Gothic style still in existence, with its triple arcades to north and
south and double lancets in the east wall. But the style is
emphatically not plain and austere. Within the church the
chapels in both nave and transepts can still be distinguished and
the position of the high altar is marked by a stone slab. In the
south transepts the tiles that once floored the whole church can
still be seen.

South of the nave is the cloister, a huge 140–foot square that
was surrounded by an arcade, part of which had been
reconstructed at the north–west corner. Along the western edge
of the cloister is the lay brothers' range, though many laymen
must have lived out at the granges or in Rievaulx village, as their
ratio to monks was sometimes as high as 4 to 1 and the monks'
accommodation is double the size of this range.

To the south of the cloister was the kitchen and a warming
room — in fact a second room, the first having, presumably,
become too small for the house. Only in the infirmary and the
warming room were the Cistercians allowed fires. The room must

Rievaulx Abbey

have been very popular in the harsh Yorkshire winters.

Between the kitchen and the warming room is the frater, or dining-room. It is a magnificent building. When the sun streamed through the tall, elegant lancet windows this must surely have been a fine place to eat, even if the meal was a simple one.

Running parallel to the frater was the monks' dorter or dormitory. This building was on three floors, as the fall of the land added a 'basement' to the two–storey building. The dorter was on the top floor, the lower floor being in part a day room, in part the novices' quarters. Off the dorter, at right–angles to it, was the reredorter or latrine, a running drain below which acted as a continuous sluice. The novices' quarters also extended below this. Since the basement of the dorter building was occupied by a tannery, the novices were thus sandwiched between a building where urine was boiled and a primitively flushed communal toilet. The novices probably had more than one reason for hoping that their novitiate would be of limited duration!

Between the dorter and the south transept were a library, treasury, parlour — the only room where conversation was allowed — and the chapter house. In the latter the monks met daily to hear a chapter from the Rule of St. Benedict, and for the Abbot to make formal announcements. Usually in Cistercian Abbeys the chapter house was a simple oblong room, and was so at Rievaulx during the first phase of building; when the Abbey was enlarged an apse, a semi-circular area, was added to the eastern end. In the west wall is a shrine believed to have covered the remains of St. William, the first Abbot.

In the south of the chapter house, beside the dorter building, was the infirmary cloister with the infirmary on its east side. In the sixteenth century the Abbot appropriated the whole of the infirmary block and converted it into a sumptuous lodge with courtyard and kitchen. It was the final act of decline from Cistercian principles and St. Aelred would most certainly not have approved.

At its height Rievaulx had 140 monks and as many as 600 lay brothers, more a small town than a religious community. The monastic houses held a position in the social fabric of the day that we can barely conceive of. The great Norman lords who were

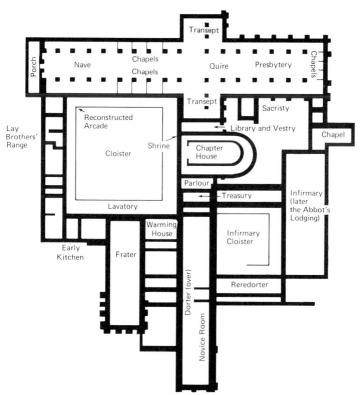

THE PRINCIPAL FEATURES OF RIEVAULX ABBEY

their benefactors were hugely generous, a generosity it would be cynical to impute solely to a desire to buy their way into heaven with a percentage of their ruthlessly gotten gains. There was genuine piety. The peasant attitude was perhaps more ambivalent. The houses represented a centre of wealth and the advantages of great agricultural and industrial improvements of the Cistercians, and the rudimentary education given by the

Benedictines were very real. Also, the peasants were still superstitious and the upkeep of the holy men was a small price to pay for their own salvation.

But by the sixteenth century the system had gone badly wrong. The Abbeys had become very rich — some individual Abbots were as rich and as powerful as the lords — and had lost touch with the ordinary folk. There were far fewer novices and many monks had allowed their devotions to lapse. When Henry VIII suppressed the houses it was not too difficult to persuade the people that the motive was to rid religion of an irreligious cancer, rather than to swell the privy purse. In the North there was more opposition than in the south. But even here at Rievaulx when the end came, in 1538, there were only 22 monks.

The lead and timber were stripped, the stonework became just cliffs, easy quarries to plunder for building material. All that remains is a marvellous echo. During his time at Helmsley, Vicar Gray tried to raise the cash needed to restore the Abbey. Perhaps just one abbey, faithfully restored, would be a good idea. I hope that if that is ever to happen, it is not Rievaulx that is chosen.

Our route does not visit the Abbey, going no closer than the River Rye bridge, but to miss out the short detour is to miss one of the great features of the walk. The bridge itself is a fine structure, but what of the river it crosses? The official view is that the Rye ran further to the north when the monks settled on their grant between river and the moor scarp. Then, on the other bank of the river, another community of monks arrived who, seeing the impracticality of having two groups so close, withdrew to found Byland Abbey a few miles to the south. The Rievaulx monks then took over the other bank and moved the river to increase the size of their land on the northern bank. Thus what is now termed a canal is, in fact, the river's original course. But is that so? The fall of the land where the Abbey stands would have been equally restrictive and might itself have been the cause of the unusual

A Rievaulx Terrace temple seen from the Abbey

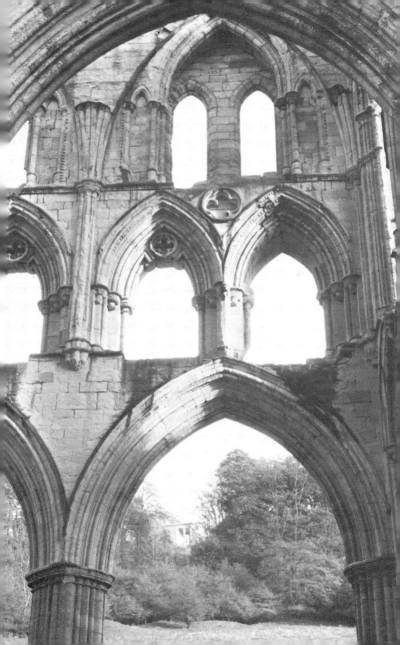

orientation, and the canals could be real, and have been dug to bring in building stone. The canal to the south does, in fact, finish near Hollins Wood where there is a quarry and, also, an incline leading down towards the water.

If the canals were dug by the monks it was a considerable labour. Another — not theirs — was the construction of the terrace and temples that lie on the scarp slope above the Abbey. These were built in the mid-eighteenth century for Thomas Duncombe and are worth a visit. The Ionic– and Doric–styled temples that occupy each end of the terrace are interesting, and the view to Ryedale and the Abbey though the trees is excellent. Both terrace and temples are administered by the National Trust.

The Hambleton Hills

Beyond the River Rye bridge the Cleveland Way continues along the road, ignoring a right turn to Old Byland and going around a conspicuous, long, left–hand bend. As the bend ends there is, at (563 845), a metalled forestry road to the right that the Wayfarer follows north–west, then west, along the stream in Nettle Dale. At (556 846) a plank bridge to the right allows the stream to be crossed, very close to where it springs from the tree roots. Go through a gate and along the track to (552 847) leaving Nettle Dale in favour of the now dry Flassen Dale. At (549 846) turn right up a small side valley and follow the track to Low Field Lane, leading to Cold Kirby.

Kirby means the farm by the church. The addition 'cold' needs no such explanation, just a windy day in mid–winter, and it becomes very obvious. But the village does not attempt to shelter itself from the elements, grouping itself snugly around its church. Instead its houses are boldly set in a string like washing on a line waiting for the wind. It is a very honest little village. Inside the church is a brief history of the manor to which Cold Kirby was attached, noting that it was owned by both orders of fighting monks, the Knights Templar and the Hospitallers of St. John, before passing into the more passive hands of the Duncombes. The church has a twelfth–century font, but dates otherwise from a mid-nineteenth–century rebuild.

The village was home to Willie Moffitt, who went missing mid–way through the funeral service for his wife only to re–appear with a huge stone grave slab he had dragged from a local gill. He had been eyeing it for years for this very purpose, he said by way of explanation.

Just beyond the end of the long Cold Kirby street and just before a lane meets our lane from the right, at the chapel, a walled lane leads off left, bending right then left and ending at a gate. Go through and follow the field track to the forestry road at (528 835). Turn right along the road past Hambleton House, a training stables for racehorses and the only connection now with

Cold Kirby

the days when Hambleton Down, to the north of us, was famous
as a race-course. Horse–racing was established here as early as
the late sixteenth century and a century or so later the course was
reckoned among the finest in England. But after 1811 other, less
remote, courses were available, and there were no further races.

At (523 833) there is a road junction. Turn left and go down to
the A170 near a hotel. Turn right and follow the main road to
(521 829). Here a road leads left, due south, towards the
Yorkshire Gliding Club, while the A170 goes due west towards
the Sutton Bank Information Centre. We bisect the angle,
heading out along Casten Dike.

The dike is one of many in the area whose origins are not
understood. Even their date is a mystery, with a variety of
suggestions from Iron Age to Roman British to medieval. The
nineteenth–century natives of Cold Kirby used to maintain they
were dug to stop Bonaparte! But as to whether they were

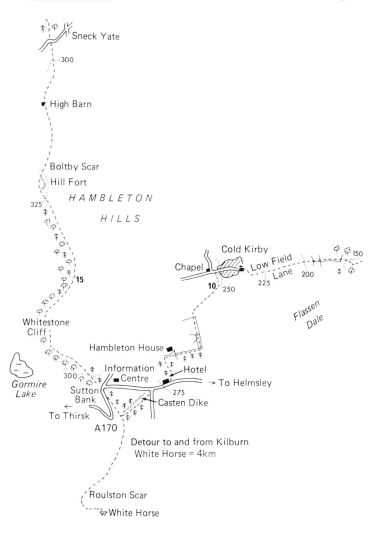

Sneck Yate

300

High Barn

Boltby Scar
Hill Fort

H A M B L E T O N

H I L L S

325

15

Whitestone
Cliff

Cold Kirby

Chapel   Low Field
              Lane
10 250   225   200   150

Flassen
Dale

Hambleton House

Gormire
Lake

Information
Centre   Hotel

300

Sutton
Bank   → To Helmsley

To Thirsk   275
              Casten Dike

A170

Detour to and from Kilburn
White Horse = 4km

Roulston Scar

White Horse

defensive, or were enclosures, no one really knows.

At the dike end is the sharp escarpment of Sutton Bank. The Way goes right, north–west, along the edge to Sutton Bank Centre, but it is worth taking a detour south to visit the Kilburn White Horse.

The White Horse was dug in 1857 by John Hodgson, the Kilburn school teacher, with the help of friends and pupils. It appears to have been cut just because Yorkshire did not have one, but the choice of slope — the scarp here is 1 in 3 — and the fact that the underlying soil is a limestone mud, not chalk, have meant that maintaining the county's only Horse is a logistical feat not too dissimilar from making it in the first place. Maintenance is in the hands of the Kilburn White Horse Association, a registered charity, who stabilise the soil, add chalk and colour wash, dig drainage channels to prevent rain erosion, and put up signs to stop people walking on the figure, a practice that leads to its rapid deterioration. Just the thought of re–painting the figure — do they paint individual pebbles or do they have a spray? — fills me with a mixture of horror and admiration.

The Horse is huge, 314 feet long, 228 feet high, enclosing an area of around 2 acres and can be seen for many miles to the south. The record distance for spotting is apparently over 40 miles. Indeed, so huge is the figure that the visitor has to go several miles away really to see it at all well. And from a distance I confess to some misgivings. Clearly it is representational, no flowing lines here as at Uffington in Berkshire and, as such, is a foal of its time. There is a Stubbs look about it. But it is more than that. The hindquarters are better than the forequarters. Did the cutters have problems with the scarp slope at the head end? Did they start at the head and get better as they moved towards the tail? Did they start at the tail and get bored as they moved headwards? Am I just being too critical?

Kilburn village is not only famous for a giant horse but for a tiny mouse, the symbol used by Robert Thompson to 'sign' his woodcarving. Thompson is world–famous now and was

The Kilburn White Horse

especially good at carving for churches. Both York Minster and Westminster Abbey have examples of his craft, as do, more humbly, Kilburn and Helmsley churches. A self–taught man, Thompson used the traditional tools of his craft, his work being notable not only for the mouse but for the ripple finish given by using a hand adze. Thompson died in 1955.

Had we been here, on Roulston Scar, 6½ centuries ago we could have watched a Scottish army under Robert Bruce pouring down off this hill. Their target was the army of Edward II encamped at the scarp base after returning from Scotland, where they had captured one lame bull before retreating. As the Earl of Warren said: 'By my faith, I never saw dearer beef.' Though it accomplished nothing, the attack incensed the Scots who followed Edward here. Some went around Roulston Scar to outflank the English. This, the surprise element and the Scottish fervour resulted in a rout. Edward, staying at Byland Abbey, finished his meal despite the attack, a foolish delay that caused him to leave the royal baggage behind when he eventually had to join in the mêlée. The king was fortunate; he made it to York but only just, being chased to the walls. Most of his army was not so lucky, being either killed or captured. That night Bruce replaced Edward at the Abbey, while his men ravaged the area.

Beyond Kilburn is Coxwold, the showpiece Yorkshire village with Shandy Hall, home of Lawrence Sterne who wrote *Tristram Shandy*. And beside that is Byland, with the ruins of another Cistercian Abbey. But all that is for another day.

We must retrace our steps to Sutton Bank, noting as we go the fine defensive position of the hill fort, the largest and strongest Iron Age fort in north–east Yorkshire. The area defended was 53 acres, certainly sufficient to paddock even the giant horse.

As we approach Sutton Bank again, look westward and towards the base of the scarp slope to Hood Grange, one of the most beautifully sited houses in the area. The house is late–seventeenth–century but the barn beside it is medieval, and records a chapter in the early history of the site. There was a hermit here, a former monk of Whitby Abbey, and later, monks came from Calder Abbey looking for a permanent site.

South of the Grange is Hood Hill, an outlier of the scarp. It has been left behind, an island of hard rock as the soft rock weathered away. The name is curious. Could it be from Hod, the ancient name for the Devil? There is a stone near by that has a 'footprint' on it that could be the Devil's. There is, as we shall see, a Devil legend associated with Whitestone Cliff; there are witches and other supernatural beings at Gormire Lake, and even a ghostly castle that used to sit on the hill.

At Sutton Bank there is a new National Park Information Centre and a view that is phenomenal: on good days it extends beyond the Yorkshire Plain to the far Pennines. The Bank is ascended by the A170 which, with its 1 in 4 hairpin bend, was used to test hill–climbers. At the top was one of the Moors' famous crosses, probably erected as a 'Thank God' where the weary traveller could rejoice in having reached the plateau.

The Cleveland Way does not actually reach the Information Centre, crossing the A170 at the scarp edge, and continuing easily along to Whitestone Cliff.

The cliff is 120 feet of vertical limestone and is well known to local climbers. Its alternative name of White Mare's Crag links it to the legend of a lady on a white mare which took fright and jumped over the cliff with her, never to be seen again. It is not for this legend that the cliff is most famous, however. A better-known story concerns the jealousy which a local knight, Sir Harry de Scroven, felt for the Abbot of Rievaulx. The knight had a fine horse but the Abbot's horse, a white one, was better. One night Sir Harry finds the Abbot in an inn (?!) on Black Hambleton and tells him that a dying man on the Moor needs him, offering to show him the way if he can borrow the Abbot's horse. At this point the story becomes too difficult for me to follow — why should the men swap horses? But no matter. The knight leads off with the Abbot close behind. Soon the Abbot overtakes him and leads the pair of them towards the cliff. Too late Sir Harry realises the danger and falls, and as he does so he looks up to see the Abbot on his horse hovering in the sky —

Two horns on the head of the Abbot were growing
And his feet cloven-hoofed in the stirrups were showing

The Devil, disguised as the Abbot, calls to the knight as he is killed on the rocks below the cliff —

> If you must play a trick
> Try it not on Old Nick.
> I'll see you below, when I visit the sick

Being limestone and a scarp slope with a base spring–line, the cliff is, geologically, unstable, and several spectacular rock falls have been reported. One of the most remarkable stories is told by John Wesley, the preacher, who arrived in Sutton–under–Whitestone Cliff shortly after the events of 25 March 1755. He reports that at first there was a great noise, and two men riding near looked up and saw 'a large body of stone, four or five yards broad, split and fly off from the very top of the rocks. They thought it strange, but rode on.' Later a larger chunk of rock measuring 45 by 30 by 65 feet came away. And then another rider 'observed the ground to shake exceedingly, and soon after several large stones or rocks, of some tons weight each, rose out of the ground. Others were thrown to one side, others turned upside down, and many rolled over and over; being a little surprised, and not very curious he hasted on his way.' The rolling over and so on continued for several days.

These events are remarkable, as are Wesley's observers who, apparently, were so unimpressed they just carried on as though they had witnessed something normal rather than something cataclysmic. Admittedly I would not have rushed to the scene had I watched a block of stone weighing many hundred tons being tossed about, but I would not have been 'not very curious' either.

Below the cliff is Gormire Lake, surprisingly one of only two natural lakes in Yorkshire. The lake, often seen from the cliff top, but difficult to reach and rarely visited, fills an ice–cut trench that was blocked off, probably, by a landslip. It is associated with many legends, as are most sheets of dark water under brooding cliffs.

It is said to cover an ancient city that was swallowed up by an

Gormire Lake from Whitestone Cliff

earthquake: the tall chimneys of the city are sometimes seen above the water when the level drops, though regrettably this undermines the legend that the lake is bottomless. The city was visited by an angel dressed as a beggar who went from door to door asking for a glass of water. At each door the angel was refused, but at last an old woodcutter and his wife invited him in and shared their supper with him. The angel blessed them and cursed the rest, so that the earth swallowed up the city except for their house. It is a nice story, but I find the angel's behaviour decidedly Old Testament.

The witch Abigail Croister, who lived locally in a cave, jumped into the lake when she was being chased by hounds and came out at a spring nine miles away. Mind you, Abigail had an affinity with water: she was once seen near Kilburn flying out of a stream on her besom. In one respect, though, Abigail was outclassed; a goose that disappeared in the lake was next seen 12 miles away at a spring near Kirkbymoorside, without any feathers.

The stories mask a quite remarkably reality — the lake has no water inlet or outlet. Possibly there is an underwater spring.

Beyond Whitestone Cliff the Way hugs the scarp edge as before. A couple of hundred yards to the east, Cleave Dike does the same and has followed us from Sutton Bank. It does not make the dikes any easier to understand, it being almost inconceivable that the whole of this scarp edge could have been one giant hill fort. Someone once suggested that the dikes were long, ancient villages. Our ancestors put roofs over them and lived underground . . .

At (505 856), at the head of Boltby Scar, there is a real hill fort for those who have avoided the temptation to leave the scarp edge at (508 853). It has been damaged by agriculture but the eastern defence of rampart and ditch is still visible. The western defence is obvious. The fort enclosed 2½ acres and within it or, more likely, within one of the three barrows that were once more obvious inside, a pair of early Bronze Age gold ear–rings were found.

Boltby, the village from which the scar gets its name, is a small,

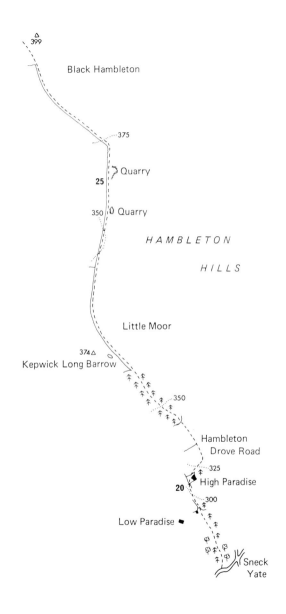

△
399

Black Hambleton

375

25 ⌀ Quarry

350 ⌀ Quarry

HAMBLETON

HILLS

Little Moor

374 △
Kepwick Long Barrow

350

Hambleton
Drove Road

325
High Paradise

20

300

Low Paradise ◼

Sneck
Yate

scarp–base weaving centre. It grew up near the spring–line and, having no church, burials were carried out at Felixkirk, a couple of miles further west. Bodies were carried uncoffined but linen–bound, a procedure which came rapidly to an end when one day a shroud ripped slightly and the cadaver started to emerge, to the horror of the mourners.

Interestingly, the next village, Kirby Knowle, also had a problem during the transportation of a body along the same corpse road. In this case the body was coffined for the trip on a warm day in autumn. At one point the bearers stopped to take a breather and to pick hazelnuts. When they came back the coffin was light: the body had gone, though the lid screws were undisturbed. The terrified men buried it regardless. And at speed.

Beyond Boltby Scar keep to the scarp edge, passing, at (507 867), High Barn Farm, which is kept to the Wayfarer's right. Keep to the middle of the next field to a gate into Sneck Yate Lane, at (508 875). Cross the lane to a path through the small forestry plantation, keeping above Low Paradise Farm to reach High Paradise Farm (503 888). What comical images these two farm names conjure up.

Keep High Paradise to the right on a track that turns north–east to meet the Hambleton Drove Road at (504 890).

A Drove Road is a track section on the British hills where, as with a Roman Road or an ancient path such as the Ridgeway, the walker really does have history beneath his feet. It is thought by many that the Hambleton Road could have been in use as early as the Bronze Age, although there is no hard evidence for its use prior to the Roman period. The Romans used Hambleton Street, although it was never a paved military road. The road crosses Scarth Nick, a glacial meltwater channel with a Norse name, although the naming does not necessarily imply a usage.

It is thought very probable that William the Conqueror came here from Durham on his way to York during the 'harrying of the North' and he encountered some real moorland weather, his personal retinue becoming detached from the main body of the army in a night–time blizzard. Doubtless the locals, had they known, would have felt such a thing could not have happened to a better king.

The Drove Road on the Hambletons

   With five monastic houses in its immediate vicinity, the road
was important during the Middle Ages and became more
important still when, ironically, roads in the Vale of Mowbray,
west of the Moors' scarp, improved. A law requiring landowners
to spend some time, at first four, later six, days annually, on the
upkeep of local roads had never been enforced. Instead the
turnpikes were created, a toll system for road upkeep that seems
to have been unpopular with everyone except the operators.
Especially badly hit were the Scottish drovers bringing meat to
England, who had to stop at every gate and waste valuable time
while their herds were counted and their tolls calculated. The
Hambleton Road bypassed all the turnpikes and became
extremely popular with the drovers, a popularity never shared
among the coaching fraternity because it was always too rough.
   Droving, the transport of meat on the hoof, had probably been
in existence since earliest times, but was most prevalent in the
eighteenth and nineteenth centuries. By that time 30,000 Scottish

A cautionary note on Black Hambleton

cattle per year were being driven to England, together with
sheep, pigs and poultry. The Scottish drovers were a rare people.
They bought their cattle in Scotland, not droving for a wage as in
some places, and sold them in England, needing, therefore, not
only to be good cattlemen and mountaineers, but excellent
businessmen as well.

Along the road drovers' inns sprang up, as did a number of
smithies. The cattle were shod for the journey, to minimise the
chance of lameness. Because of their cloven hooves, each animal
needed eight shoes, and the smiths had to be both highly skilled
and very brave — just imagine trying to nail eight shoes onto the
hooves of a recalcitrant Highland bull. Frankly it is something I
would rather imagine than do! It was not only the cattle that were
shod, stories being told of geese and turkeys' feet being fitted
with pads, or of being coated with a tar–and–sawdust mixture. A
big drove, cattle, pigs, poultry, perhaps 2 miles in length, must
have been a fine sight.

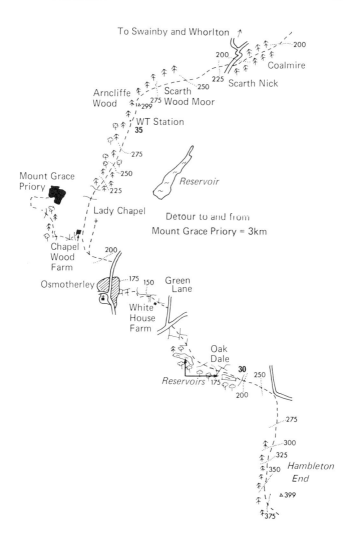

To Swainby and Whorlton

Coalmire
200
200
225
Scarth Nick
250
Scarth
Arncliffe
Wood Moor
Wood
275
299
WT Station
35
275
250
Mount Grace
225
Priory
Reservoir
Lady Chapel
Detour to and from
Mount Grace Priory = 3km
Chapel
Wood
Farm
200
Osmotherley
175
150
Green
Lane
White
House
Farm
Oak
Dale
30
250
Reservoirs
175
200
275
300
325
350
Hambleton
End
△399
375

The view down Oak Dale

The Drove Road is continuous from Scarth Nick to Sutton Bank, but we follow it only as far as (480 009) giving 4 miles of well–defined track across some of the finest moorland in the National Park. At (495 902) we pass the base of Steeple Cross and then at (492 904), behind the wall to the left, lies one of the few long barrows in Yorkshire, the Kepwick barrow. When excavated in the nineteenth century this Neolithic grave, now 110 feet long, 30 feet wide and 4 feet high, was found to contain 5 skeletons.

At (491 919) we pass the ruins of the Limekiln Inn, a drovers' inn but with a name associated with another passing trade, the packhorse carriage of lime crushed from the Hambleton oolitic crust. With the coming of canning and then railways, the drovers

deserted the road and the inn lost its custom. It was the end of a
most interesting way of life: the drovers brought colour to the
neighbourhood and were, in the main, well liked, acting as
postmen and news–carriers, and being fair game for the thieves
who frequented Black Hambleton, waiting for the well–paid
cattlemen returning to Scotland.

Beyond the Limekiln at (491 932) bear left (north–west) rather
than taking the north–bound track that eventually wheels
eastward and way off–route. It is safest just to keep to the wall,
and that has its compensations: the view of the Vale of Mowbray
and beyond is superb. At (479 959) the Wayfarer reaches the road
but does not follow it, going north–west immediately. Now we
cross Jenny Brewster's Moor, and also pass her spring. The
name, as we shall see, is probably associated with moorland
smuggling.

The descent into Oak Dale is a fine piece of walking, although
the going can create a few problems for the unwary. Ahead is a
reservoir, the first of two that supply Northallerton, and we are
aiming for the wall that skirts its northern shore. Stay high above
Oakdale Beck and head for the north–east corner of the reservoir
where the feeding beck is crossed. Go through a small wood to
the northern shore. Follow the shore–line and then a track to the
deserted Oakdale Farm (469 964), where a lane is taken north–
westward to the road at (465 968). Turn left (south–west) and
after about 50 yards right (north) into Green Lane. At (465 970) go
left (west) towards White House Farm which is passed on the
Wayfarer's left. A path leads down to Cod Beck which is crossed
by a footbridge at (461 972). Beyond the bridge a stepped path
climbs the steep, wooded western bank of the Cod Beck Valley,
leading to open pasture land which is crossed using, if need be,
the tower of Osmotherley Church as a guide. Head just north of
the church to read a narrow hedged lane turning into the aptly
named Back Lane. A narrow path opposite leads past the old
Methodist Chapel, through a passageway and out into the village
square.

Osmotherley

Osmotherley is one of those many villages found throughout Britain that are romantically named, grouped around church or cross, and that have a timeless charm. It is as though the tides of ages have lapped but gently over them, never strong enough to erode or silt up the essential nature of the place.

In the case of Osmotherley the name is linked with as romantic, though sad, a tale as we shall hear on our journey. The Saxon King Oswald had a son, Oswy, whose death by drowning on a specific day was foretold by a seer. In horror, the young prince's mother took the boy to spend that day on Roseberry Topping, a remote, dry peak to the north–east of our village. There, in the summer sun, she lay down to rest, exhausted by her anxieties. When she woke the prince was nowhere to be seen and, at last, his mother found him lying face down in an unsuspected spring. She brought him here, to a village then called Teviotdale, where he was buried. Soon after the grief–stricken queen died and was buried beside her son. And so, once again, young Os-by-his-mother-lay.

There is no evidence for any occupation of the village site much before the coming of the Normans, though there is a cross–shaft and a tombstone at the church that are believed to be Anglo–Danish. The village occupies an isolated, though sheltered, spot, tucked under the moor, near no obvious moorland trackway or exit of a plateau–splitting valley. The villagers' hold on life must have been precarious, an existence made much less easy by the Norman king's harrying — Domesday Osmotherley, as with so much else, is described as 'waste', wasted by William's armies, and by Scottish raids. A raid in 1315 so devastated the village that it was granted exemption from taxes for four years. Legend has it that men from the village, acting as moorland guides, had led the army of Robert Bruce astray, leaving his knights floundering in bogland when they suddenly extinguished their torches. There is no end to this story, the villagers' loyalty to the Norman kind being the point of the tale. But if there is any truth in it, it takes no genius to work out that the end would have been swift and savage retribution by the Scots.

As if all this were not enough, the Black Death decimated the village a generation later. It is a sad story — though, of course, no sadder here than elsewhere —with harrowing tales of isolated families living in fear and not daring to help their neighbours, whose deaths they could surmise only by noting that no smoke now rose from their chimneys.

The village escaped the Civil War but was stricken in the mid-eighteenth century by a bovine equivalent to the Black Death, a cattle distemper so severe it moved the vicar to note that 'The Lord moves in mysterious ways, but some of us wish that he wouldn't be quite so mysterious about this plague. If he goes on with it we shall be beggars, that's a certainty.' The parish clerk wrote a psalm asking God to relent and all the farmers came one Sunday to sing it. It is told that all sang from the heart except five, who stood and cried. What is not told is whether the anthem had the desired effect.

But the bad times were now at an end. An alum works opened in Oakdale in 1752 — we shall discuss alum mining later, at a more appropriate point on the Way — producing over 80 tons annually from three boiling pans, although it lasted only 25 years, being just a bit too far from the coast, and there were local lime kilns too. The quarries produced stone for the railways as well as for crushing, and moorland stripped of heather by lime now fed sheep. By 1800 linen weaving was a high–earning local industry, with many mills set up along Cod Beck. One, Walk Mill — 'walking' was part of the cloth fulling process — was closed as lately as 1948.

Osmotherley, with its new–found prosperity, became the local capital and its two-day annual fair — which sometimes lasted a week! — was *the* event. At it Toby Douthwaite would play the violin continuously, night and day, a task he performed for over 50 years, due in no small part to his reputed ability to continue playing while drunk, asleep or both.

The village is well worth a walk around, having a fascinating collection of old cottages. It is also interesting in having a bend on each of the streets that meet at the square, so that when you look

up them you cannot see out of the village, the street being closed
off by the houses going around the corner. Was this a deliberate
attempt to give the place a folded–in appearance to encourage a
cosy neighbourliness, or was it chance?

Those interested in the history of religion in England will also
find Osmotherley rewarding. The parish church of St. Peter is a
fine building with parts dating from Norman times, around 1190,
but having been much, though not too savagely, restored in the
late nineteenth century.

The village also has, in the Catholic chapel in the Old Hall just
off the square, a link with the history of that faith in England. As
we shall see when we continue our journey, the Lady Chapel, a
little north of the village, was a centre for pilgrimage at a time
when to be Catholic was to risk death. An Armada beacon was
positioned locally, a fact not calculated to improve the lot of local
Catholics, and yet despite all this the Walmesley family had a
chapel in the upper part of the Hall. It is likely that the altar was
easy to dismantle and hide, and the chapel was easy to disguise,
but it was nevertheless a remarkably brave act to worship in quite
so public a spot.

We have already passed the Methodist Church on our way to
the village square, built originally in 1754 and enlarged a century
later. The early establishment is due to the close association of
John Wesley with Osmotherley, which he visited 17 times, the
last in 1784 when he was 81, though it is worth noting that
Wesley lived to be 88 and was active until a few weeks before his
death. John was fifteenth of the 19 children born to Samuel
Wesley, rector of Epworth, Lincolnshire, and his wife Susanna.
John was born on 28 June 1703, narrowly escaping death six years
later when the rectory burnt down. He went on to become a
gifted scholar of Christ Church, Oxford, was ordained and then
formed with his brother Charles and a group of Oxford students a
society called by other students the 'Methodists' because of their
regulated way of life. During this period Wesley adopted the
habit of rising at 4 a.m., a habit which stayed with him until his

Osmotherley

death. The two brothers went to Georgia to minister to the
settlers, but Charles soon returned, plagued with ill–health. John
followed a little later, more plagued by the irritation his regulated
life provoked in the less well–disciplined frontiersmen. In 1738
John took up the evangelistic life for which he is famous, a life to
which he remained dedicated for over 50 years.

Wesley's message was that the road to God was a hard one,
and the history of the world is that those who make life difficult
for people are not welcome. Ultimately even the established
Church closed ranks against him and he founded his own, taking
for it the original Oxford joke name.

Wesley was invited to Osmotherley in April 1745 by Father
Peter Adams, a Franciscan — certainly an odd introduction —
and was well received by a crowd who gathered to hear him
preach at 10 p.m. He went to bed at midnight, rose as usual at
4 a.m. and preached once more at 5 a.m., many of the crowd
having waited up all night to hear him again. In March 1747
Wesley preached in the church but by April he had been banned
from it, the local vicar having been roundly abused for offering
him the earlier privilege.

It is widely believed that Wesley preached his first sermon from
the old barter table, the stone slab raised on short stone legs that
stands beside the restored cross. If so, the table has had a
chequered pattern of use; it has supported market produce,
preachers, and coffins on their way to church.

But the market produce the slab supported was everyday stuff,
which is more than can be said for some of the goods that came
this way when smuggling was the main trade on the coast the
other side of the Moors. Then there were kegs in ponds and
pigsties, and just about anywhere else one could be hidden. Or
so it is said. The trade probably gave the name to Jenny
Brewster's Moor, and to Jenny Bradley's Stone that we shall pass
later. There was, apparently, an old saying, that Billy was going
and Jenny was coming, a coded message for the men of the
village having gone to fetch contraband. Possibly Jenny was from
gin, and Brewster from brewing. Bradley? Well, just part of the
disguise, perhaps. Alternatively, either name could derive from a
long-forgotten witch. Osmotherley has long been a place where

the supernatural mixes with the normal. Those going down to Thimble Hall should beware; it is haunted by a man on a white horse. Apropos of nothing, Sir John, one of the local family of Colville who lived at the Hall, gets one line in Shakespeare's *Henry III*. If you are only going to be given one line in history, that is no bad place to have it.

The Cleveland Way leaves Osmotherley northward, on the road for Scarth Nick and Swainby. Just beyond the village at (457 976) Rueberry Lane bears left (west) and we follow it around the snout of Rueberry Hill towards Chapel Wood Farm (452 980). At the farm a path going south–west leads to Mount Grace Priory, while just above the farm the track splits, the left fork being ours. The right leads to the Lady Chapel, a site certainly worth the detour of a couple of hundred yards.

Mount Grace Priory

The inn in Osmotherley that bears the name Queen Catherine is said to be named after Catherine of Aragon, a popular lady in a North that resisted Henry VIII's changes to the religious order of things. There is a local legend that the Lady Chapel, also occasionally called Lady Catherine's Chapel, was built with money obtained from the queen to house Thomas Parkinson, a Thirsk hermit. Parkinson, a Bedale man, lived in Thirsk with his wife. When their first child was stillborn the midwife buried it in the garden in a shallow grave from which the crows dug it. The horrified couple, seeing this as a sign from God, devoted themselves to monasticism, the wife becoming a nun, Thomas becoming a hermit in Thirsk church porch — an unlikely spot in which to find solitude. Sir James Strangeways petitioned the queen to build the chapel and here Parkinson lived for 12 years, occasionally visited by his wife. If the story is true the patron's choice of incumbent was not a wise one. When Mount Grace Priory was dissolved Parkinson had to leave the chapel, which may have come under the control of the Prior, and he wandered about, living on charity until he arrived in Bridgnorth where he married again (bigamously?), became a tailor and then a hermit at Stow-on-the-Wold. When his history was revealed he was imprisoned.

The Parkinson story is one oddity. Following the Dissolution the chapel became a place of pilgrimage, illegal pilgrimage since those who came were Catholics. The magistrates at Northallerton fined and imprisoned as many as they could catch, but still they came. Why?

It was said that miraculous healing took place here, that a child apparently dead became well, and that the miracles were the result of the chapel's relics. Whose remains were they? One idea was that they were those of Margaret Clitherow, the wife of a York butcher, who used to shelter priests in a room in their house in the Shambles. For this 'crime' she was executed in 1586, crushed to death under a stone; at the time of her death she was

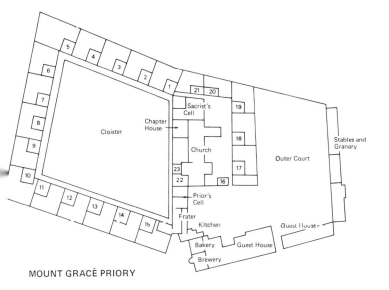

MOUNT GRACÈ PRIORY

pregnant. The story has her body brought here for secret burial, but that does not really seem all that likely: it is an awfully long way to carry the crushed body of an executed person in secret. Another version of the story names the relics as the bones of St. Cuthbert, brought here secretly from Durham at the start of the Reformation. That seems more plausible — the bones would have made a smaller parcel — but there is no real evidence that St. Cuthbert's remains are not still at Durham. So the mystery remains.

The House of the Assumption of the Most Blessed Virgin and St. Nicholas of Mount Grace at Ingleby, to give the Priory its full name, was not started until 1398, very late in the monastic history of England. The Carthusian order for which it was built had been founded in 1184 by St. Bruno at the Grand Chartreuse in Provence in a deliberate attempt, as we have seen, to return to the solitary life that had been the norm for the early monastic hermits. As such, the Priory consisted of cells in which the monks lived alone, the house itself existing only for reasons of economy and security, since the solitary holy man had not been as well protected from thieves and murderers as might have been expected. The first two English charterhouses, as the Carthusian settlements were called, were built in Somerset, one in the late twelfth century, the other in the early thirteenth century. The order did not expand further until the mid-fourteenth century, when, probably in reaction to the lack of monastic rigour in the established orders, the number of charterhouses rose from two to nine, Mount Grace being the eighth. Its founder was Thomas de Holland, the Earl of Kent, whose grandmother, Joan, the Fair Maid of Kent, was mother to King Richard II. Unfortunately for the Priory, de Holland fell into disfavour when Richard was deposed, and was executed in 1400 when he rebelled against the new king, Henry IV.

The re-allocation of de Holland's title and land caused the new charterhouse much aggravation, disputes on revenues from granted lands — now re-granted by the new duke — carrying on for a decade or more but being finally resolved. By the mid-fifteenth century the Priory was a comparatively rich house.

When Henry VIII dissolved the houses the Carthusians opposed him manfully. It would be wrong to say that the other orders did not, but the ease with which most monks in the communal houses were absorbed into ordinary life suggests that they had attracted some whose monastic commitment was not total but who had been tempted, in part, by the relatively easy life that the houses by now offered. In sharp contrast, the enclosed and solitary life of the charterhouse was hardly likely to be chosen by anyone except a committed monk. Three of the nine Carthusian Priors were executed for refusing to accept Henry's supremacy, and in the London charterhouse a third of the monks shared the same fate. At Mount Grace two brothers were imprisoned in 1534 for refusing the oath of Henry's Act of Succession, though ultimately, in December 1539, the Priory was

Mount Grace Priory

surrendered. Prior John Wilson was given a pension but was arrested later, implicated in the Pilgrimage of Grace. He was released at length and became a monk at the Sheen charterhouse which was re–founded under Queen Mary.

Within the ruin of the charterhouse the most obvious difference between the Priory and, say, Rievaulx Abbey, is the individual cells around the cloister, a sharp contrast to the communal dormitory and refectory of the Cistercians. Each of the cloister cells was about 27 feet square and on two storeys. The ground floor had an entrance lobby, a living room with fire, bedroom and study, with passageways to a garderobe and to the monk's garden where he grew herbs. No second storeys have survived, but it is thought they were workshops.

The charterhouses were the publishing houses of their day, the monks copying old books and manuscripts. In comparison to the cold, draughty rooms of Rievaulx, where the monks were required to remain silent to dispel the presence of other brothers, this does not seem so bad. But just how alone the Carthusians were can be seen from the right–angled serving hatch in the cell walls off the cloister. The angle is there so that the monk could receive his food without ever seeing the person who brought it. How many of us would relish years of such a self–imposed solitary existence?

The monks did come together occasionally. There is a frater, a dining room, because there were communal meals on feast days. There is also a chapter house for similar occasions, and a small, simple church, because part of their worship was also communal. These buildings are all contained within the south wall of the cloister, which also holds the Prior's cell and three cells so tiny as to be barely usable.

The private house now to the west of the church occupies the former kitchen and guest rooms of the Priory. To the south of the church was a courtyard, formed, on its southern side, by granary buildings.

As the visitor wanders about, the austerity of the monks' life is somehow apparent. Even at the Dissolution, when the richness of some houses made Henry VIII's task easier, Mount Grace was a place of poverty. There is an other–worldliness about the site: it is difficult to forget that the Carthusians wore large cowls over their heads — the archetypal ghostly monks.

Mount Grace Priory is a little off our route but should be visited. It is the most extensively preserved charterhouse in England, which alone would make it worth the detour. But, in addition, its quiet setting has more to say about the spirituality and less about the architectural magnificence of English monasticism.

The Cleveland Hills

Whether the Wayfarer has visited the Lady Chapel or Mount Grace Priory, he leaves Chapel Wood Farm, following a wall across 3 fields. At the exit from the last field into a plantation, turn sharply right and uphill to meet a wall on the ridge. The wall is followed past the TV booster station, on the site of what was Brass Cottage, built here as an artist's studio. One look at the view is enough to see why. Beyond the TV masts is a trig point at the summit of Beacon Hill.

Beacon Hill was Kop Keld Hagge where an Armada warning beacon was built ready for possible invasion. It is also the start of the Lyke Wake Walk, perhaps the most famous of the named walks that have been 'created' on the North York Moors. The Lyke Wake route crosses 40 miles of moorland to reach Ravenscar on the coast. We shall reach the same point but will have travelled further. We shall also take longer than the 24 hours that is all the Lyke Wake Walkers are given if they are to qualify as 'dirgers', official members of the Lyke Wake Club. The origin of the name and the journey across the moors is the Lyke Wake Dirge, an ancient dialect poem that was certainly sung in the sixteenth century and probably earlier. The word 'lyke' derives from the same root as 'lych' in lych–gate, meaning a corpse, the dirge being a funeral song, dating from the time when the Moors' people were used to the idea of carrying bodies along corpse roads for burial. It was believed that the soul of a dead person had to cross the Moors to reach Paradise, and in the crossing it had certain obstacles to overcome. On Whinney Moor, for instance, the soul met a man carrying shoes. If the departed had, when alive, given a pair of shoes to a poor man, the soul could retrieve them to protect its feet from the thorns of the moor —

When thoo fra hence art passed
Ivery neet an all,
T'Whinney Moor thoo cumst at last,

An Christ tak up thy soul.
If iver thou gavest hosen or shoon
Ivery neet on all,
Clap tha doon an put em on,
An Christ tak up they soul.

At last the soul reached the Bridge of Dread, where it was asked if, in life, its bearer had given money to the poor. If the answer was yes then the soul could reach its goal. If not then it would 'doon tummle towards Hell fleems'.

The idea for the modern walk and club came from Bill Cowley of the Swainby area. As a test piece for the walker it was a good idea, being a very fine walk. As a fun idea it also succeeded at first. But now the walk is so trampled it has become a mud track in places, spoiling what it sought to enjoy. The damage is mainly but not exclusively due to organised charity–type walkers. For them the competition, not the walk, is the important thing. There are now races along the route, a fastest time quoted and so on, and the debris at the road–crossing 'feeding stations' is a disgrace. I am not impressed by talk of man–the–walker being just another version of man–the–competitor. There are sufficient areas available for competition, contrived or otherwise, without turning the hills into a race–track.

A few tens of yards beyond the trig point the route turns right (north–east) through gates and leads downhill towards the road at Scarth Nick.

We have now turned the corner in our journey, having reached the north–western corner of the Moors. Now we are heading for the sea, although in front of us at the moment all we can see are the northern scarp slope of Carlton Bank and the moorland outlier of Whorl Hill. The route is obvious, the pathway through Clain Wood beyond Scarth Nick being quite clear from our vantage point on Scarth Wood Moor.

To our left there are fine views over the newly revealed Vale of Cleveland towards the Tees, above the trees of Arncliffe Wood. The Arn–cliff itself is lost among the trees: it was once famous as the haunt of eagles. On a good day Great Whernside and Mickle Fell, to the west, can also be seen.

At Scarth Nick — Scarth is Norse for a notch — we reach the famous Ice Age overflow channel and meet again the Drove Road that we followed across Black Hambleton. The road rises up from Swainby where, in the last quarter of the nineteenth century, one Henry Cooper was born, a man who grew to a sadly unaccredited height of 8 foot 6 inches, which would have made him taller than *The Guinness Book of Records'* tallest Englishman by many inches. Henry was, equally sadly, kept as a circus freak, touring the USA with Barnum and Bailey, and dying at only 32.

Next to Swainby, at Whorlton, the Moors' approach via Scarth Nick was defended by a castle, built by Robert de Meynell around the end of the fourteenth century. It is now little more than rubble though still with part of a gatehouse. An earlier de Meynell, Stephen, endowed a hermit's cell here at the Nick itself, and history records that another member of the family, Alice was rewarded by a gift of 4 shillings from Edward II for singing to him when he stayed at the castle.

The Scarth Nick road is steep, but is it really as bad as Arthur Young, the eighteenth-century traveller, would have us believe? The way is 'beyond all description terrible' as you descend 'through such steep, rough, narrow, rocky precipices that I would sincerely advise any friend to go a hundred miles to avoid it'. I am always perplexed by such descriptions, and not just by doubts about whether Young offered different advice to those who were not his friends. The traveller–writers of that time seemed to find horror in what we now consider commonplace, and dread in what we seek when we go out into the hills. Have times changed to such an extent that we can now tolerate easily precipices that they had to draw the blinds on their coaches to avoid seeing for fear of sickness and fainting? Or were the descriptions deliberately exaggerated for a reader who wanted to gasp and utter oh, gosh! as he sank back into his chair and reached for his brandy? That cannot be the whole story, because these odd descriptions persisted after the generality of English gentlefolk started to sally forth to the wilder spots in search of the

The Cleveland Way and Lyke Wake Walk at Coalmire

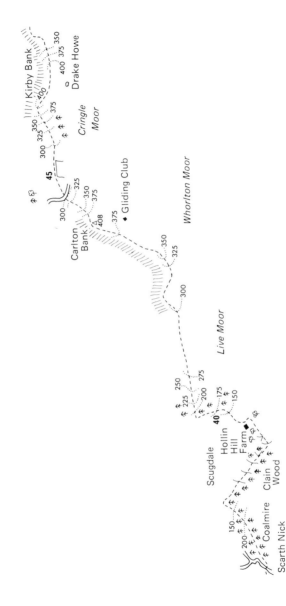

Picturesque, and a thrilling Tour. It really is an intriguing question.

Beyond Scarth Nick the obvious pathway through Clain Wood that we saw from Scarth Wood Moor is taken. Do not be tempted to go north at (481 009) but keep on the well–trodden route north–east. The whole route from Beacon Hill to Round Hill, some 11 miles, is in fact very well beaten, because the Cleveland Way follows the Lyke Wake Walk.

At (482 009) turn sharp right (south–east) near a gate and follow a path that contours the side of Scugdale. At (490 003) the route goes sharply left and downhill. The turn is through a gate and is obvious but for those not sure, it is at a point directly opposite Hollin Hill Farm (492 005) on the other side of Scugdale. Cross the field to a gate and on to a path that fords Scugdale Beck. At a track turn left (north) on a long bend past Hollin Hill Farm to a junction (493 007) where there is a telephone box. Go across and through the gate to take a path going north–east, with the field fence on your left. On your right are the remains of the Carlton Iron Ore Co.

The path splits at the far side of the field. Turn left (north) along the forest edge to (494 013) where the break in the forest is used to climb up eastwards to Live Moor. The climb is steep and can be slippery, but the view from the moor above is very good, especially back down into peaceful Scugdale. It is difficult to envisage the valley filled with the bustle and noise that must have been associated with the extraction of over 60,000 tons of iron ore.

There is a well defined path over Live Moor, or rather, along its northern limit and on to the trig point above Carlton Bank. I find it difficult here to avoid the temptation to cross the ridge of Live Moor to the woodland on its southern edge, a plantation that takes its name from the valley running down off the eastern edge of the Moors. This is Snotterdale.

Crossing the Live Moor ridge the walker also crosses the Moors' watershed. It is possible (just!) to stand with one foot in land drained to the Tees, one in land drained to the Humber.

Back on the route, a little caution is needed when approaching the trig point. On the moortop there is a gliding club, and while the gliders themselves make a fine sight, the released tow from

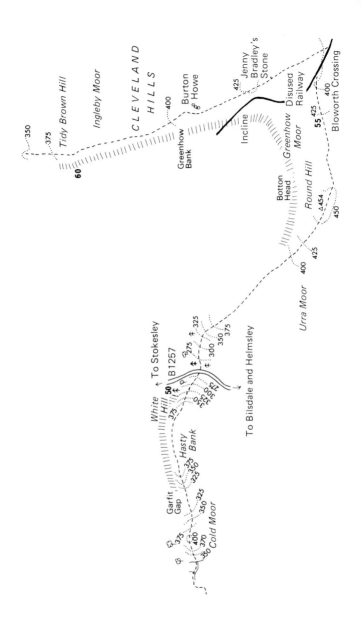

them comes down with a crunch and a lot of leg–entwining cable attached.

By the time the trig point itself is reached the view can be enjoyed in safety. Dominating the scene is the sculpted peak of Roseberry Topping, a moment of truth for those feeling the pace, since we shall stand there. But remember how good it will feel to do so and look back to here.

The way off Carlton Bank is straightforward, going north–east to the road at (522 030). Do not be tempted too far down at first: the old alum works can make the going tricky. The stone at the roadside is the Three Lords' Stone, marking the old boundary between the estates of the Duncombes of Helmsley, the Marwoods of Busby Hall and the Aisleburys of Pangdale, all of which have weathered less well than the stone.

Beyond the road the way ahead is again obvious, rising up on to Cringle Moor, 'cringle' from the old word for a circle, an indication of the shape of the hill rising to Drake Howe rather than from allusion to any ancient stone circle. The Cleveland Way does not visit the moortop, but does reach a standing stone, seat and panorama dial set on the edge of Kirby Bank. The stone is another boundary marker, the seat is a memorial to Alec Falconer, a respected local rambler. The dial points out some of the further peaks that good viewing weather will reveal. Cross Fell is, perhaps, the best example. The weather will need to be exceptional to see it, but it has been seen. The more obvious points that can be picked out are Cook's Monument on Easby Bank, on the route, and the villages of Great Broughton, beside which is the site of a medieval village, and another Kirkby.

Beyond Cringle Moor go down to a wall at (544 032) but do not climb it. Instead, go north along it then follow it around west to find a gate at (545 033). Go through this, up right and then west and up to the summit of Cold Moor. On a windy day it can be a relief to find some moderate shelter in Gorfit Gap before the climb up Hasty Bank. There is light relief here, too, the Wainstones, eroded blocks of bare rock that are very popular with climbers. The name is interesting. Some have contended that it just means 'stones by the way', but a way along the scarp edge does not seem very likely. The miners, for instance, looking for ore in the hills here, had their track lower down, out of the wind. Another version of the name was 'wain' deriving from the Saxon 'wanion', to howl. That could imply that the stones were seen as stones of lament, an interesting link with the Lyke Wake Walk which the Cleveland Way is still following. Perhaps, though, the howling was the noise of the wind through these natural organ–pipes. Snowdonia has its 'Castle of the Winds', a similar jumble of stones named from their effect on the wind. Hereabouts bare rocks are a novelty, and the wind noise could have been equally novel.

Beyond the Wainstones the route is easy to follow over the flat top of Hasty Bank, with the rock outcrop of Raven's Scar to the north. On the eastern downslope the Way is equally straightforward, descending to the wood edge which is followed, finally, by an enclosed pathway to the road at (573 033).

The road here links the Cleveland Plain with Bilsdale and Helmsley. The woodland to the north on Clay Bank is a fine place with bluebells in spring. It is easy to linger, particularly as there has been a lot of climbing since Osmotherley. But Round Hill is the final climb and is a rewarding summit. From there the Way is level or downhill as we turn north to drop down into Kildale.

Go straight across the road through a gate and along the northern field edge to a stile. Now keep close to the edge of the forest, following what was once a paved path up through some rock outcrops and out on to Urra Moor. There a firebreak is joined and followed to the summit of Round Hill. The trig point here, at 1489 feet, is the highest point of the North York Moors and, therefore, of our walk, and we have climbed 3500 feet from Osmotherley. These are two good reasons why we should stop and contemplate all the surrounding moorland.

The Moors have never accepted man's presence without putting up a fight, and the land is littered with the remains of farmhouses that were ruined after the hearts of their last inhabitants had been broken. But, as always, some held on, and a special breed of people arose who could tolerate the hardships.

Hang-glider over Carlton Moor

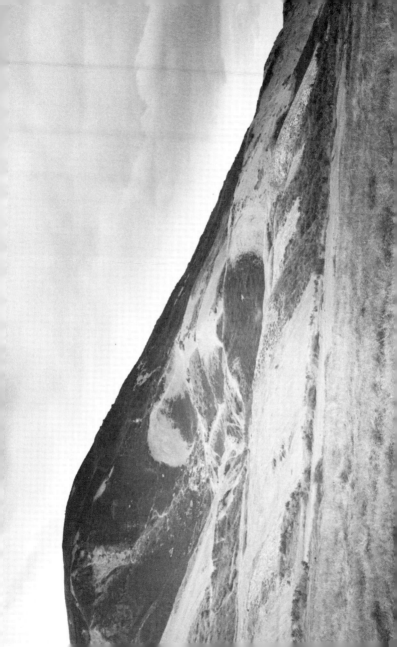

They were philosophical about the weather: there is a local saying for when the rain falls in sheets or the blizzard blows thick and fast — that it is all God's weather, though this is not some of his best. And they understood the land — 'There's a lot of land that's called bad, that's only short of muck.' They knew nature too —

A swarm of bees in May is worth a load of hay
A swarm of bees in June is worth a silver spoon
A swarm of bees in July isn't worth a fly

— though it is odd that they believed that radishes rubbed on the hands made a person immune to an adder's bite.

Perhaps such herbal remedies were the superstitious lot of an introspective folk. Certainly they were superstitious, believing in all sorts of bogles and hobs on the Moors. They believed in the Gaabrel Ratchet, the corpse hounds who hunted the Moors above head–height looking for souls. If they went over your head you would die. From the noise the hounds were supposed to have made it would seem that the moorfolk were hearing a nightjar, but that does not explain the story.

Their houses had witch posts to protect them. These were fixed from a beam, usually in the kitchen, and no witch could pass them. At the top there was St. Andrew's Cross and below it a series of horizontal bands. The post was always of rowan, and they worked —

Oh Master, oh Master, we can't do no good
She's got a witch cross made o' mountain ash wood

— one witch said to the Devil. Sometimes a sixpenny piece was kept in a hole in the post, to make sure that the farm butter could not be bewitched.

The posts were necessary, witches were everywhere. On the Moors, as in many other remote areas of Britain, one witch frequently turned herself into a hare, being recognised when the

The Cleveland Way over Battersby Moor

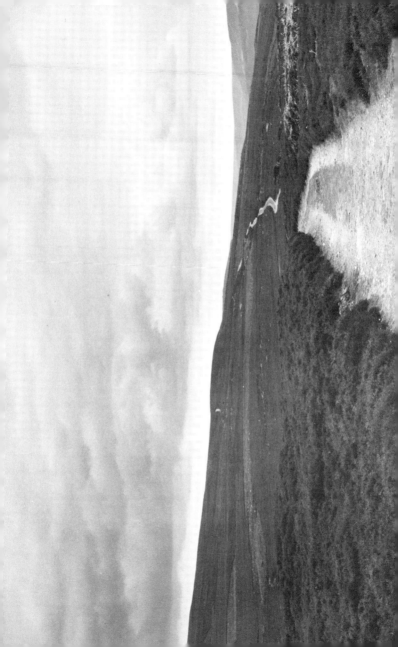

hare was chased by a dog and the old woman emerged from a thicket limping, she said, from a fall, but with teeth marks on her leg.

If it all seems such a long time ago, it is worth noting that the last (known!) person to perform magic by sticking pins into a bullock's heart died only in 1926.

But it was not all black art. The Moors bred characters with an earthy pragmatism and humour. One local tale concerns an old farmer who lay dying in a downstairs room while his wife discussed with a neighbour how to dispose of his effects. The old chap, aggrieved at one idea, offered an opinion of his own. His wife turned quickly — 'You get on with your dying, we'll do the talking and arranging.'

On a lighter note, I love the story of a squire's man sent with a brace of pheasants to the local vicar. The man knocked at the vicarage door and when the vicar opened it, he thrust the pheasants at him with an abrupt 'Pair of birds for you.' The vicar tut-tutted about the man's lack of manners, took the birds and offered an on–the–spot lesson. Changing places, the vicar knocked and said — 'Squire's compliments, sir, and would you accept this brace of pheasants.' 'Thank you, my man,' said the man–turned–vicar, 'and here's half–a–crown for yourself.'

In terms of its non–human life the Moors are equally sparsely populated. The soil is poor and vegetation types limited and this, combined with the harsh winters, keeps down animal life. But there is dwarf cornel among the heather, bog myrtle in some of the wetter areas, and a variety of trees in the sheltered dales. Farndale, which starts a couple of miles east of Round Hill, is named for the fearn, the alder, but is famous for its daffodils.

Butterflies are never abundant, but many species have been seen. Strangely, the green hairstreak is among the commonest, and it is an insect that few non–specialists know at all. Despite the climate there are adders and slow-worms, as well as the more expected hares and foxes.

There are few permanent residents among the birds, only the

The Cook Monument on Easby Moor, beyond Kildale

carrion crow, red grouse and meadow pipit coming easily to mind. Spring brings a predictable increase, the golden plover and merlin being particularly welcome. The winter visitor might just see a snow bunting, a hooded crow, a Montague's or hen harrier. In the dales the list increases, though it does not include a genuine rarity.

To the north of Round Hill and below the steep scarp of Botton Head are two farms. One is Midnight, so–called — or so it is said — because the scarp slope wrapped around Ingleby Dale shut out the sun and it was always that dark. The other is Cloggers' Hall, which is close enough to the name of the Bill Tidy cartoon characters to confirm the prejudices of most southerners. It is actually named for the clogs made in the middle of last century for railway workers.

An old trackway went down Botton Head, linking the northern and southern side of the Moors at this narrow part of the plateau, using the spur of gentler land that is still called Turkey Nab, from thurkil, an ancient local name for a track.

Not so old, but equally interesting, is the old railway that the route meets at (612 017) or at (609 020) if a short cut is taken. This is the Rosedale Railway. It climbed out of Rosedale at Bank Top, up a 1 in 3 incline not negotiated, it need hardly be added, by the engines, only by the loaded coaches that were gravity–hauled up, full of Rosedale iron ore. At the top the coaches were steam–hauled along elegantly sweeping lines — to reduce the need and, therefore, the expense of bridges — that when followed today, though the lines themselves have gone, still offer wonderful views into Rosedale and Farndale before crossing the boggy moor east of Round Hill to the edge of the Ingleby incline. Here, again, the coaches were gravity–hauled, the incline being less steep, 1 in 5 in places, but mostly 1 in 8 to 1 in 11.

The line, opened in 1861 to haul the newly discovered Rosedale ore to the Tees, still draws the railway enthusiast. It is engineering for the connoisseur, though even the amateur can marvel at the hardiness of the men who built and operated the line, particularly in winter. Some of the workers obviously felt the cold; a clutch of cottages at the head of the Ingleby incline was called 'Siberia'! It is not hard to see why. They found snow near

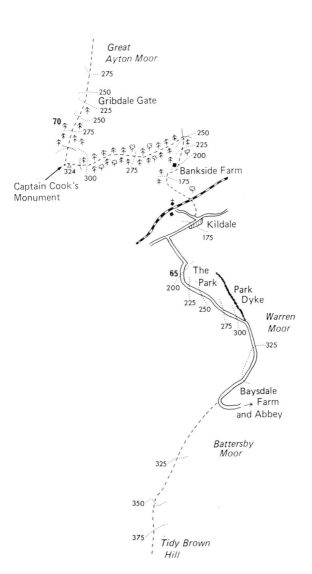

Great
Ayton Moor

275

250
Gribdale Gate
225
70 250
275

250
225
200

Bankside Farm

324 300 275
Captain Cook's
Monument

175

Kildale
175

65 The
Park
200
225 Park
250 Dyke

275
300 Warren
Moor
325

Baysdale
→ Farm
and Abbey

Battersby
Moor
325

350

375
Tidy Brown
Hill

the line in mid–August in 1895, and it was 30 feet deep in 1917.

The gravity–hauling technique, empty coaches being pulled up by down–going full ones, was fraught with danger. The hauling was done by one wire rope acting around one drum and if – or rather when – it failed, the results could be catastrophic. The Ingleby incline is not far short of a mile long. Imagine heavily laden ore trucks going down a 1 in 8 slope for a mile. Assuming they stayed on the track, however, I imagine it was only necessary to switch the points for them to career on to Middlesborough.

Over its lifetime the railway hauled 10 million tons of ore, but by 1926 it was carrying in one year what it had once carried every fortnight. On 11 January 1929 the last load went down the Ingleby incline. Behind it the moorland track was being lifted. As a final insult the weather froze the track–removing engine's whistle. The other engines could not manage the incline. They were dismantled and lowered the same way as the coaches had been. On 8 June 1929 the last engine went down and the Moors returned to a solitude they had not known for 70 years.

Near the Round Hill trig. point is the Hand Stone, an old–fashioned waymark pointing the way to 'Stoxea' (Stokesly) and 'Kirbie and . . .', erected around 1711 when the Northallerton courts decided that the North Riding needed signs. Further along the Way, following the firebreak eastward, is the Face Stone, a far older standing stone with a rough, but fierce, carved face. The face looks Celtic, though it may be a much later, though still old, boundary marker. Further along again, and to the left, is a section of paved trackway, probably built for packhorses. It was once much more extensive, but has been much plundered for local building. It was also used by the smugglers en route for Osmotherley, and is still known as Smugglers' Trod.

At (605 016) a short cut across now well-drained Moors leads directly to the northbound path at (611 022), avoiding the walk to Bloworth Crossing (616 015). I use 'Bloworth' because that is how

View back along the northern scarp slope from The Peak

the O.S. and many locals have it, but I am aware that many people call this spot Blowith.

At (611 022) is Jenny Bradley's Stone. Beyond at (608 033) is Burton Howe, one of the most spectacular of the Moors' Bronze Age burial sites. The howes, the local word for such mounds, are four Bronze Age round barrows, each still impressively large despite weathering. The most southerly, with a diameter of 50 feet and 8 feet high, is the most impressive. It is revetted by a stone kerb and contained a wood-roofed burial chamber, the roof supported by four posts. Our ancestors certainly had an impressive eye for a site. There were, almost definitely, more reasons than one for building here, but the site satisfies two probable ones in wonderful style. The mound is a lasting and visible reminder of those buried here, even if we have lost their names; and if their spirits are with us still, they have a fine view to rest their eyes on. All along this northern leading scarp the views towards Ingleby Greenhow, a picturesque old village, are excellent.

We continue on our moorland road to (602 050) where, at an old stone signpost, we turn half right (north-east) to go through a gate. The gate has no fence either side, but it would be churlish to walk around it!

Ahead now is Battersby Moor which is crossed at (608 067) by Cross Dyke, another poorly understood dyke. At (611 070) we reach the road to Baysdale Farm, to the east of us at the head of Baysdale itself. Beyond the farm is the site of Baysdale Abbey, though nothing now remains of the twelfth–century Cistercian nunnery. The nuns must have been a hardy band of women. Baysdale has all the remote beauty expected of a Cistercian foundation, but it must have been a cruel place in winter.

We follow the road all the way to Kildale, turning right at (603 092) when we reach a road junction. On the first downhill section we have followed the line of Park Dyke, a dyke believed to have been cut to enclose a deer park for Ingleby Manor. If that is the case it was civil engineering on a massive scale.

Kildale is a quiet spot, with no pub and no shops other than the Post Office, but astonishingly it is on the railway and has a station

Kildale Church

in as strange a spot as could be imagined in this age of Inter–City, when it seems a statutory requirement that people by the tens of thousands should live in a place before British Rail realise it exists. The line also gives Kildale Church one of the most delightful approaches of any that I have ever visited. At the end of a lane leading to the station and a farm, a gate gives access to a narrow wooden footbridge over the railway. At the bridge end is another gate to the churchyard. The iron road has certainly preserved the seclusion of this church.

St. Cuthbert's church was re–built in 1868 and during foundation-digging work, 7 or 8 bodies were unearthed. They were laid head to foot along an east–west line and with them was a quantity of weapons — swords, axes and daggers — in iron and bronze. The swords were laid across the skeletal legs in the manner of pagan weapon burials.

There is evidence for Norman occupation of the dale — the remains of a motte and bailey castle are found west of the church — and Pevsner wondered whether the font was Norman. Since the Normans usually settled on existing sites and built on already sacred land, it does not seem likely that the church site has been Christian for centuries. It is conjectured that the ancient burial could have been early Danish at a time when the Danes were embracing Christianity. Sadly, the whole burial was ransacked and lost.

For the rest, Kildale is a typical small North Riding village with a history rooted in weaving mills based on moor–stream power. In a flash flood during a summer storm one mill was entirely washed away. To prevent a recurrence and to give a more constant driving head, dams were built, the collapse of one of which destroyed the Bleach Mill, on the site of which Bleach Mill Farm now stands, to the west of the village.

Captain Cook Country

To leave Kildale the Cleveland Wayfarer goes towards the church and station, missing a view of the village 'big house', Kildale Hall, a fine late Georgian mansion. After about 30 yards turn right (north) along the gated road to Bankside Farm (604 101). The farm was constructed on the plan of a Danish longhouse, where the men of the 'hundred' — an ancient 'parish' that contained a hundred farms — would meet. A long hearth would stretch down the centre of the room and the men would sit facing it, their backs to the longhouse wall, to hold a meeting, a 'thing', to discuss local business. The Tynwald, the Parliament of the Isle of Man, has this Danish word as the basis of its name.

Continue up the hill beyond Bankside Farm and through the forestry to (605 105) where a gate left (west) allows access to a track through the forest to the open land of Easby Moor, and the Cook Monument.

James Cook was born on 27 October 1728 in a two-roomed thatched cottage at Marton, then a village but now engulfed by Middlesbrough. His father, James senior, was a farm labourer with Scottish ancestors; his mother, Grace, was a local girl. The house where James was born no longer stands, though a granite vase marks the spot where the young boy lived for eight years, learning to read with the help of a neighbour, his father being illiterate.

In 1736 James senior was offered a better job, and the family moved to Great Ayton, the village most associated with Cook's boyhood, lying below Easby Bank where the monument stands. The family lived in a cottage the position of which is marked by an obelisk of Australian granite, taken from a site near where Cook landed on that continent. This cottage does exist, but it needs more than an afternoon trip to see it. It is in Fitzroy Gardens, Melbourne, having been dismantled stone by stone and re–erected there in 1934. Even the creepers that grew around the cottage were dug up, moved half–way across the world and re–planted. The purchase was not without difficulty, the last

owner having stipulated that the cottage should not go outside England when she heard of American interest in it, but being persuaded to alter this to not outside the Empire. The Fitzroy cottage has, so I am told, a lintel dated 1755, long after the time James had left Great Ayton, but it probably only signifies restoration work, and it is known that James visited the village after that date.

At Great Ayton James impressed his father's employer, Thomas Skottowe, who paid for the boy's schooling and then, in 1745, arranged for him to become an apprentice in a grocery and haberdashery shop in Staithes, a North Sea village that we, too, will visit. The shop is no longer there: the sea nibbles away at the coast constantly, and included in one mouthful was William Saunderson's shop.

At Staithes James obviously fell in love with the sea, and when his apprenticeship was completed, after three years, he joined the collier fleet of the Walkers, a Whitby Quaker family. His first voyage was in the somewhat inappropriately named, in view of the owner's religious leanings, *Freelove*. On the collier he learned quickly, fast becoming a mate, and what he learned of the Whitby–built ships as well as of the sea was to stand him in good stead many thousands of miles away from the North Sea coal routes. By 1755 the Walkers were prepared to give Cook a command, but war with France was clearly in the offing and James enlisted in the Royal Navy instead. For two years he served on two ships, the *Eagle* and the *Pembroke*, that formed part of the naval blockade of the French coast. While on the *Pembroke* he came to the attention of the captain, John Simcoe. It is not hard to see why. At that time the crew of the Royal Navy's vessels were largely press–ganged men, which made Cook, who was not only willing but able, a very notable exception. In addition he was bright and eager to learn and under Simcoe he became an expert navigator and hydrographic surveyor. General Wolfe's capture of Quebec in 1759 was due in no small part to the surveying of a channel up the St. Lawrence river by Cook when his tour of duty

Bankside Farm

on the French blockade was over.

In 1762 he married Elizabeth Batts but left her alone almost immediately to survey the Newfoundland shore–line. While there he saw and recorded a solar eclipse, his report to the Royal Society being so well received that he was offered command of the *Endeavour*, a ship sailing for Tahiti to observe the traverse of Venus across the sun. The *Endeavour* was a re–fitted, re–named Whitby collier and Cook must have thought he had come home, except that the Pacific bore little relation to the North Sea. The ship was three–masted, 106 feet long, displacing 366 tons, a very small ship to go so far for so long a time. I wonder how they all got on, captain, crew, and Joseph Banks and Daniel Solander, the botanists who accompanied them.

The trip was a success but better was to follow, for Cook opened secret orders at Tahiti telling him to sail south and explore. On 7 October 1769 Cook sighted North Island, New Zealand. The new country had been seen before, a century before, by Abel Tasman, but Cook was the first to survey it; and it was he who discovered that there were two islands, separated by a channel now called the Cook Strait. The islands were, Cook thought, suitable for settlers 'should this ever be thought an object worthy of the attention of Englishmen'.

There is a monument near Kaiti Hill to commemorate Cook's landing on 8 October 1769, and a statue on the hill itself similar to the one at Whitby. There is a Whitby in New Zealand, named by Cook, who also named Young Nick's Head, the spit of land first sighted by the expedition. The spotter, and winner as a result of a gallon of rum, was Nicholas Young, a 12–year–old!

After landfall in New Zealand Cook went on to survey the eastern shore–line of Australia, and named New South Wales. In June 1770, to his utter astonishment, Cook's ship struck something while apparently sailing in 17 fathoms of water. To Cook's list of accomplishments was added the discovery of the Barrier Reef. Now the Whitby–made ship and captain came into their own. Cook beached the *Endeavour* to carry out repairs, the ship being strong enough to cope with the stress, Cook being good enough to minimise it.

Cook returned to England in mid–1771 and was promoted to

Captain Cook's Monument

commander, but was able to spend little time with his wife before departing on a second voyage to the South Seas in 1772. Again a pair of Yorkshire ships, re–named *Resolution* and *Adventure*, was taken. This time Cook became the first man to cross the Antarctic Circle, though the chief merit of the trip was less in the exploration, good though it was, but in Cook's anti–scurvy diet including lemon juice. It was for this work that he received the Royal Society's Gold Medal and was elected a Fellow, when the expedition returned in July 1775.

Within a year the newly promoted Captain Cook was off again, taking *Resolution* once more and *Discovery* to the Pacific. On this occasion, however, the main purpose was to search for the North–West Passage around Canada's northern shore, but from the Pacific side. Cook found the Bering Strait — a duplicate of the Whitby statue stands at Anchorage, Alaska — but with winter coming he was unable to push far north against the pack ice. Instead he returned to the Pacific, to a place he had discovered and called the Sandwich Islands. There, in December 1778, he landed on Owhyhee, that we today call Hawaii. The islanders greeted Cook as a god, but in February 1779 a boat was stolen from *Discovery*. Unable to locate it, Cook decided to take the island king hostage against its return. In a confrontation on the beach Cook still held sway over the islanders as long as he faced them, but when he turned to shout orders to his boats, he was stabbed in the back. It was 14 February 1779 and Cook had just passed his fiftieth birthday.

It was a sad end to a great career of exploration, a sadness only heightened by the knowledge that though Cook and his wife had had six children, none survived infancy. Of the man himself, it is sometimes hard to catch a glimpse, except in terms of his achievements. There is the famous story of the 'South Seas Shilling', a coin minted by the South Sea Company which Cook reputedly stole or exchanged at the shop in Staithes, but it is almost certainly apocryphal. There are, too, stories of his womanising, which also seem at best exaggerated. It is hard to

The route to Great Ayton Moor

escape the idea, when reading of the man in the few texts that talk of him, that he was just a normal, rather taciturn man possessed of great common sense, a gentleness towards his fellow men, certainly in relation to his crew, and with a courage and inquisitiveness that were allowed full rein because of the times he lived in. Let that suffice.

The monument on Easby Moor was erected in 1827 by Robert Campion, a Whitby banker, and it has been restored twice, most recently in 1960 when it was struck by lightning. This latter event is not mentioned on the monument's plaque, though much else is, the inscription giving a brief description of the life of both Cook and the obelisk. At 60 feet, it is no small tribute, and acts as a beacon to the Moors walker for many miles in all directions.

To continue from the monument, go slightly east of north on the well defined path through the forestry that now covers Little Ayton Moor, and down to the road at Gribdale Gate (592 110).

Across the road the Way continues northward, with the wall at the scarp edge on your left, across Great Ayton Moor. The views westward to Great Ayton are wonderfully extensive, but the eye is drawn at all times to Roseberry Topping, the shapely peak we are approaching. The Wayfarer could, at any point, strike north–east and up for the top of Great Ayton Moor, beyond which the route could be rejoined at Black Nab. There will be few, however, who will forgo the chance to climb such a distinctive peak, which looks huge despite being 10 or so feet lower than the ground Cook's Monument stands on. At (588 128) the reason for this becomes apparent. Roseberry Topping is an outlier, separated from the closest approach of the moorland plateau by a 1000–yard wide, 325–feet deep notch.

Water is the major erosional force at work on the North York Moors, the water acting not only on the rock surface, picking away at individual grains of sandstone, but also carrying away the grains to act as 'shot–blasting' material further down, and preventing any re–stabilisation by this actual removal of material. But the erosional effects of water are irregular; water only flows in

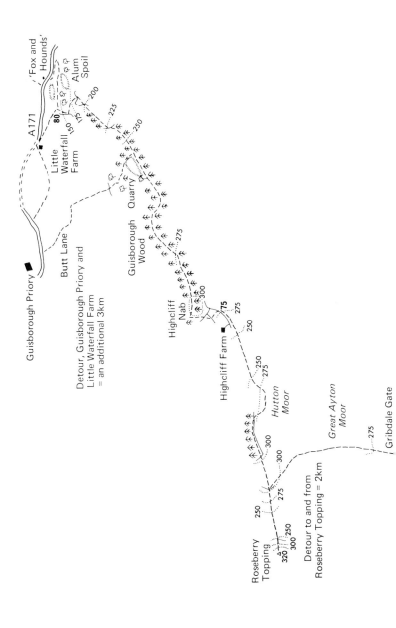

Guisborough Priory

A171

'Fox and Hounds'

Alum Spoil

200

Little Waterfall Farm

80

150
175
225
250

Butt Lane

Detour, Guisborough Priory and Little Waterfall Farm = an additional 3km

Guisborough Wood

Quarry

275

Highcliff Nab

300

75
275
250

Highcliff Farm

250
275

Hutton Moor

300
300

250

Great Ayton Moor

275

Gribdale Gate

275
250

300
300

Roseberry Topping

320

Detour to and from Roseberry Topping = 2km

streams, so the sculpting is uneven. Other erosional forces, basically the weather, are more even but much slower. Ultimately, if streams undermine some areas, causing collapses, the weathering produces a regular, rounded hill, just as with Hood Hill out beyond Roulston Scar and the Kilburn White Horse. The newer and therefore more irregular Roseberry Topping had its unevenness accentuated early in its life by a hard sandstone cap, and later in its life by the quarrying of the last two centuries.

But the hill's importance to local life, beyond its aesthetic and recreational uses, goes back beyond quarrying, although it was a quarryman who unearthed the oldest remnants of man's association with the hill. He found stone tools, axe–heads and scrapers, suggesting not a tool factory but a defensive site. The hill is well suited to such a use, as it has its own water supply. The Danes called the hill Ohensberg, Odin's Hill, suggesting either that it was sacred or was believed to have had a supernatural birth. The modern name derives from that Danish name.

Next came Prince Oswy, as we saw at Osmotherley, who found the natural spring. Later the spring was believed to have healing powers — 'out of the toppe of a huge stone neare the toppe of the hille drops a fountaine which cureth sore eyes, receavinge that vertue from the minerall'. There are those who have been to the hill and not seen the water. Clearly they were most in need of it!

The water was good enough for other things too. A century ago the local village youth gathered to 'drink the simple beverage and to join in a variety of rural diversions'!

The hill not only healed, it prophesied —

When Roseberry Topping wears a cap,
Let Cleveland then beware a clap

In the last quarter of the last century someone noticed that the

Thunderclouds above the northern scarp slope

hill, or at least the part below the hard, sandstone cap, was solid ironstone, and quarrymen set about the task of taking the hill out from under the cap. An aerial ropeway sent the ore down to Ayton and the railway for Middlesbrough, but that was too slow, and a narrow–gauge line was laid in to the northern foot. By 1912 two trains a day were needed to take the hill away. But no one had thought about the cap, and the straightforward need to jack things up if you are going to undermine them. In that year the top of the northern flank collapsed into the quarried workings. No one was injured, more by good fortune than good management, and work carried on. Fortunately by 1929 the operation was no longer economic and the quarrymen went away, leaving the hill scarred but still standing.

The view from Roseberry Topping is, because of its position, magnificent. John Walker Ord, writing in the early part of the nineteenth century said: 'The prospect from the summit combines at once the extreme of beauty and sublimity . . . mountains, moors, rivers, oceans with a vast and almost absolute infinity of intermediate scenery; towns, villages, halls . . . steeples . . . with forests, woods, groves, corn fields, pastures, hedgerows, green lanes, these . . . constitute one of the noblest scenes which it is possible for the mind of man to conceive.'

The description is a bit over–the–top for modern tastes, perhaps, but Ord has captured the essence of the panorama. He would be displeased with the uprooting of hedges on the Plain to the north, and with the advance of the Ayton and Guisborough dormitory estates towards the hill, but he would still recognise the view.

Roseberry Topping from the north-west

Guisborough Priory

Whether the Wayfarer has climbed Roseberry Topping or not, he will have reached (588 128). Go slightly north of east, over the top of Newton Moor, on a distinct, if narrow, track to the forest edge at (591 129) where a gate gives access to a forestry road. Follow this to (598 130) where a trackway comes up from the north and leads off southwards across the Moors. This is an old moorland road from Guisborough Priory, and we follow it for 200 yards to (599 128) where a track leads left (east). In high summer the bracken here can make the track a bit awkward, but the Way is easier to follow once the stone walls of Highcliffe Farm have been reached, at (602 130).

Follow the wall almost all the way to the forest edge, keeping close to it so as to avoid the boggy ground that is the last remnant of an Ice Age lake. At (611 135), one field from the forest edge, go left over a stile (north–west) and on to a gate. Here turn right (north) to join a forest track leading up through the trees to the rocky top of Highcliffe Nab.

The view north from the Nab towards Middlesbrough and, more north–west, to the coast, is spectacular, though not as extensive as that from Roseberry Topping. Interestingly, John Walker Ord found himself unimpressed by the southerly view: 'All is bleak and desolation; black heath stretching to the utmost boundary of vision.' It is strange that a man who could wax so lyrical about the view to the Plain could feel that way about the moorland prospect. So while he would be less than pleased about the loss of hedgerows he would doubtless nod with approval at the trees that now block out the southern Moors.

The route east from the Nab lies within Guisborough Wood, along one of many paths that criss–cross them. When we reach the A171 at the Fox and Hounds (642 158) we will have descended the scarp slope, and the moorland section of the Cleveland Way will be finished. It is a pity we do not leave the Moors along a more satisfactory piece of the pathway. But we do not, finishing with a whimper what we started with a bang.

There is only one definitive right of way eastward through the wood and this is partially marked with acorns on stones. In essence the track we want is the third highest of three that contour the scarp slope. At several points paths head downhill (north) to Guisborough and its Priory, which is well worth a visit, but they tend to require a good deal of suburban walking.

The best route to follow is the track that leaves the Nab's eastern edge, going eastward. After half a mile the track goes downhill (north–east), bearing right twice to avoid direct drops into Guisborough, and then contours around in two sweeping arcs, first right, then left, to the top of a disused quarry at (629 145). At the far end of this (632 146) a pathway downhill (north–west) leads to a lane that reached the A171 at (619 159).

Alternatively, to continue, go ahead where the path leads downhill — it also leads uphill (south–west) to the Moors — to the elbow of the forestry at (639 154) where, with the third field on your right, you see a building about 100 yards ahead. Here go through a gate and across the field to the farm road (640 155). Turn left (north) and down the road. It is gated, and about 100 yards beyond the gate at a wooden hut on the left, turn right (north) and through the small wood. It is now necessary to pick a route eastward and down through the maze of alum spoil heaps to the main road and the inn.

Guisborough Priory is the third of the four monastic houses we visit and is the most incomplete. What exists comprises only a few stones of the north wall of a range of storerooms, bits and pieces of the church and its magnificent east wall, rising almost 100 feet and containing a window that would have been 56 feet high and 23 feet wide. From this window all tracery stone has gone though it is still an impressive sight. But the little that does exist is well set on beautifully tended lawns and still represents a haven of solitude from the bustle of the next-door town.

The Priory was founded by Robert de Brus, probably the most important landowner in Norman north–east Yorkshire, around the year 1129, and was very richly endowed from the start, with an immediate grant of 10,000 acres around the site itself. This Robert was the second of his name. The sixth disputed with the Balliols the crown of Scotland, and the eighth achieved the

wearing of it, being the Robert Bruce who was victorious at
Byland, on our route, and, more famously, at Bannockburn. He
is, of course, the man who watched the spider spinning another
web, though frankly I consider that, quaint as the story is, any
man capable of murdering a rival in church had precious little to
learn about resolve from a spider. There is a legend that the bones
of the Scottish king still lie within the Priory church.

By contrast to the history of the founder's family, the history of
the Priory itself is very tame. It is, as someone noted, a story of
'dignified mediocrity'. A few minor incidents are known in its
400–year history, but the Priory had to wait for the Dissolution
before something out of the ordinary occurred. A couple of years
before the surrender, the Prior, James Cockerell, was replaced by
Robert Pursglove, a man more in sympathy with the king's aims.
Cockerell became implicated in the Pilgrimage of Grace and was
one of those executed at Tyburn in 1537. In contrast, Prior
Pursglove surrendered the house on Christmas Eve, 1539 and
retired on a very reasonable pension.

One other incident of note had occurred. On 16 May 1289 a
plumber was called to repair the lead on the roof of the south
transept. He left his 'soldering iron', a pan full of live coals, on
the roof beams when he had finished, with instructions that his
two apprentice boys should clear up and dowse the pan. This
they did not do, and in the ensuing fire the roof lead melted,
pouring into the nave and igniting it, so that the whole of the
church was destroyed — not only the structural fabric, but
chalices, ornaments, statues, vestments and library as well. It
was a disaster from which the Priory did well to recover.

The Priory has, of course, its share of legends. Its wealth gave
rise to a story that an underground passage led from it to
Tocketts, to the north, and that in it a raven guarded a chest of
gold. But best of all I like the legend that the ghost of a black
Canon walks the ruined Priory at midnight on the night of the
first new moon of the year. Not only is he seen but he is heard, as
he lets down a ghostly drawbridge over a long–gone moat. So

Highcliff Nab from Guisborough Priory

famous did this legend become that on one such night in the early 1960s an estimated 500 people turned up to witness the apparition. Everybody who was anybody was there. Except the black Canon, that is.

The town beyond the Priory ruin existed before the house was founded, though its prosperity eventually depended upon it, and was greatly enhanced by a grant of fairs by Henry III. Naturally, the town name is older than the Priory, too, and is pronounced 'Giz' not 'Guys'. At one time the Priory name was spelt 'Gis' not 'Guis', but the longer form now seems to be accepted as standard. Guisborough is now a small market town grown big to house employees of ICI Wilton, with a claim, disputed by neighbouring Skelton, to having been the capital of Cleveland. But do not be put off by the dormitory estates; there are cobbles still in the old town, which maintains its character.

Those who have visited the Priory can return to the Way by following the A171 eastward to (623 160) where a path off right (south–east) is followed back to the main road at Little Waterfall Farm (632 159). From there a path does lead off south of the A171 into the alum tips, but the Fox and Hounds is only half a mile or so along the main road, so it may be the lesser of two evils.

As we cross the main road to reach the inn, we leave the North York Moors National Park, though we shall return to it again on the coastal path section of the walk.

The Cleveland Way goes west along the A171 from the Fox and Hounds, cutting the journey of anyone who has been to Guisborough Priory by 100 yards, to reach (641 159) where it turns right (north) up the western edge of a quarry to a stile. Now skirt the quarry's northern edge to (640 161) where, at the field edge, the Way turns sharp right (north). Go up to a gate, pass through it and turn right (east) along the wall and on to Airy Hill Farm (646 167) from where Airy Hill Lane, now tarmac, is followed into Skelton Green.

Where the lane meets the main road through the village go over this and through a gate to reach another tarmac lane leading into the newer, more industrial, town of Skelton, removed from

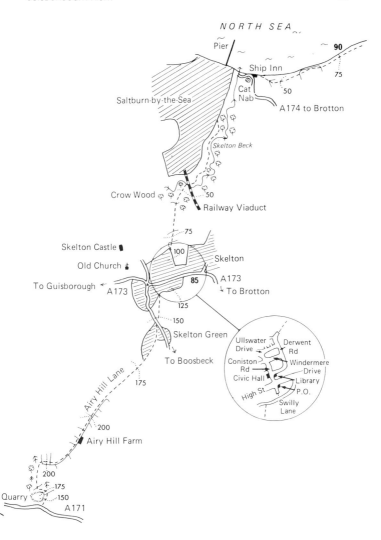

NORTH SEA

Pier

Ship Inn

90

75

Cat
Nab

50

Saltburn-by-the-Sea

A174 to Brotton

Skelton Beck

Crow Wood

50

Railway Viaduct

75

Skelton Castle

100

Old Church

Skelton

85

A173

To Guisborough ←   A173

↓ To Brotton

125

150

Skelton Green

To Boosbeck

Airy Hill Lane

175

200

Airy Hill Farm

200

175

Quarry

150

A171

Ullswater
Drive

Derwent
Rd

Coniston
Rd

Windermere
Drive

Civic Hall

Library

High St

P.O.

Swilly
Lane

the medieval green and also from the famous castle and old church site a little way west along the A173 to Guisborough.

It is probable that Robert de Brus had a castle here, and that from here the expedition to Scotland was made when land there was acquired. This land led to the successful claim of Robert Bruce to the Scottish crown, but long before that the family suffered from divided loyalties. At the Battle of the Standard, for instance, de Brus and his eldest son fought for England while a younger son fought for Scotland. The younger boy was captured and sent by his father, as a captive, to the king, who had the wisdom to send him home again.

Later the history of England may have revolved around this spot because legend has it that the barons met here to agree their declaration of rights and liberties later signed by King John at Runnymede.

The castle that now stands to the west of the village dates from around 1800 despite the castellations. Lawrence Sterne of Coxwold wrote part of *Tristram Shandy* here, the book having a reference to his host, the eccentric John Hall–Stephenson. Hall–Stephenson founded a local Hell–Fire Club with Sterne as a member, and wrote a book, *Crazy Tales*, that has the castle as its frontispiece and contains the couplet —

Over the castle hangs a tower
Threatening destruction every hour

which has little literary merit, but does indicate his sadness over the state of the building, which he attempted to repair.

Between the castle, now in private hands, and the road is an old church, built just before the castle's restoration but now in a dangerous state of dilapidation. It apparently contains a three–decker pulpit, though it would be foolish to test the truth of this.

For the rest, Skelton is a village grown rich comparatively recently on ironstone, with buildings functional rather than ornate. It is chiefly Victorian, though we leave it through an

The old church, Skelton

estate that is much more modern.

The lane from Skelton Green reaches Swilly Lane, where we turn right (north–east). A few yards along, opposite a seat, steps lead down to a short lane to the main road. Go across and on down Coniston Road opposite. Now either go right beyond the library into Derwent Road, or reach that road by taking either of the next two turns to the right. Whichever way is taken, the end of Derwent Road is reached. Go through the gate and head north across the field. The path is obvious now into Crow Wood and down wooden steps to Skelton Beck. Directly under the tremendous 780–foot–long railway viaduct, cross the beck on a footbridge at (661 201).

The railway viaduct outside Saltburn

Saltburn–by–Sea

Beyond the railway viaduct the path turns up and left (north) and can be followed directly into new Saltburn at the Y–junction of Marske Mill Lane and Victoria Road, the latter being where the Youth Hostel is situated.

Alternatively, and much the better, is to go forward (east) where the lane swings left at (662 203) to join a walk through woodland and on to the Rose Walk in the Valley Garden. This is a very fine entrance to the town and also very appropriate, as all the coastal villages we shall visit have grown up at points where the becks draining down from the Moors reach the sea. Skelton Beck flows in what must have been an excellent wooded valley before man arrived, but has now been transformed, in its upper reaches, into a semi–formal garden of superb colour in spring and summer. The Italian Gardens can be visited before the Rose Walk, but either way it is a good walk. In its final yards the valley has a miniature railway, boating lake and a nice, high–up, spidery ironwork bridge, but before that we have left the park to reach Glenside. Here go right and follow the road all the way to the sea, or turn off left at Balmoral Terrace or at Marine Parade, to visit the new town.

The town's name implies an ancient founding, when people lived by the beck, the 'burn', to pan salt from the North Sea for trading inland. The oldest part of the town, on our way out, has nothing of that age, but we shall pass the remains of a Roman signal station on Huntcliff, the huge cliff that dominates almost every view eastward from Saltburn.

The first mention of the site dates from 1215, when a hermitage here was given to Whitby Abbey. By the early nineteenth century it was, according to John Walker Ord 'a small hamlet, containing about 16 houses, situated on the sea and under a mountain . . . the massive overhanging cliffs of Huntcliff tower proudly into the heavens, assuming a most sublime and terrible aspect when wrestling with the sea'.

Ord's hamlet was collected around the Ship Inn under Cat

Nab, a 200–foot–high mound of glacial boulder clay that delights children with its steepness. The Ship is most famous for the part that it played in Saltburn's major industry in the last half of the eighteenth century — smuggling. Around 1750, tea in England was so heavily taxed that, depending upon its origin, it cost between 12 and 35 shillings per pound. In tax–free Holland it sold for 7 pence per pound, so not surprisingly at that time it was reckoned that of the 4 million pounds of the tea sold in England annually, three–quarters was smuggled. It always strikes me as interesting that tea, not French brandy or kegs of Hollands, was the main money–spinner for the smuggler, but in fact smuggled goods covered a wide range, with Englishmen setting up in business in Holland to supply the Yorkshire coast. Distilleries were built to make brandy: one produced 3 million gallons each year at around 5 shillings per gallon, in comparison to £1 a gallon here.

Loading at the continental ports, and on the sea, the contraband and its smugglers were safe enough: the Dutch and French wanted the trade, and the sea was a big place. It was the men in ports such as Saltburn who took the risks.

There were occasional fights at sea, as the off–loading boats were attacked by revenue cutters, and these battles became furious when the smugglers armed themselves, particularly those men who were not locals looking to supplement their normal wage, but were part of organised crime syndicates. Some of their names have come down to us — 'Stoney' Fagg and 'Smoker' Browning — but these were not lovable rogues. Inland they might offer a farmer a small keg to forget a packhorse train crossing his land, but equally they might beat him senseless, steal his wife and cattle, and fire his cottage. David Pinkney, a Robin Hood's Bay smuggler, boasted openly of his deeds, knowing full well that the local constable would not dare attempt to arrest him. Ultimately a troop of dragoons was taken to Baytown and stayed there until 1830. Horace Walpole noted in 1752: 'It is shocking to think what a shambles this country is grown.' It was an apt choice of words, for he had just seen 17 men hanged for smuggling. It is all a very far cry from the romantic myth.

At the Ship Inn it was John Andrew, born in Scotland in 1761 but living here with a local wife from 1781, who was the famous smuggler. The tales are legion: there was a path hewn through solid rock from the inn to Huntcliff to take the packhorses; Andrew had a horse always ready saddled in the cellar of a house at the top of the cliff; twenty packhorses could be hidden in the secret passages of the inn; contraband was hidden near a water wheel next to the inn and when a Preventative Officer went to search, the water was allowed in, almost drowning him. And so on.

Andrew became Master of the Cleveland Fox Hounds at one stage in an effort to establish himself, but was caught eventually, failed to pay a huge fine and died in prison. Today the Ship is one of many inns rejoicing in the title 'Best Pub in Yorkshire' even though it no longer has 'Fat Rascals', the small hot currant cakes it was once famous for offering with tea.

The new town, Saltburn–by–the–Sea, was built on the northern side of Skelton Beck as lately as the mid–nineteenth century, a piece of straightforward entrepreneurism by Henry Pease. He realised what had happened elsewhere — the growth of the seaside resort — and the advantages of the railway, extending the line from Redcar to service his new town. Not everyone agreed with him. One local maintained that he 'lived in the neighbourhood, and it is a nasty, bleak, cold place, and the sand is horrid'. On the latter point I believe the local was quite wrong — the sand is flat and very long, long enough to have once been home to car trials and to have been considered for Malcolm Campbell's 'Bluebird'.

As if to deny the first suggestion, that the spot was cold and bleak, Pease built his new resort right on the headland. The air was 'invigorating'; it was 'like wine'; I did not realise before I came here that anyone had used these phrases except in sarcasm. Saltburn was to be the gem of North Sea resorts, and the cluster of grid–like streets were given appropriate names — Amber, Pearl, Diamond . . . There was a short, covered line linking the station with the Zetland Hotel, so that guests could travel

Pier and rack railway, Saltburn

virtually all the way to their hotel door under cover — the Prince of Wales came that way. There was a cliff railway and a pier.

The pier was 1250 feet long in its heyday, but was cut in half by a colliding boat in 1924. Today it is only a shadow of its old self, the only survivor of six original Yorkshire piers. The town's popularity has shrunk, like the pier, and it seems, at least on the promenade, a sad, slightly confused and dishevelled place. A board warns that it is dangerous to eat cockles, mussels and periwinkles found on the shore. The notice speaks volumes. Mind you, in the old days the inhabitants would have had a cure for an ailment brought on by eating dubious shellfish. They could cure cramp with rings of lead from coffins; fits with woodlice in a tin; and thrush by burning scarlet cloth and blowing the ashes into the mouth.

The Cleveland Way leaves Saltburn beyond the Ship Inn, taking a path behind it and climbing up Huntcliff, our first clifftop walk. Route–finding from here to Filey is made easier by the Way being coastal, but take great care if you decide to walk any sections on the beach itself. The tides are quick and aggressive, and the clifftop not always too easy to regain. Huntcliff is a case in point. It is 'full of craggs and steep rocks, wherein meawes, pidgeons and sea–fowl breed plentifully'.

At (685 220) the most northerly point of the walk is reached. From here it is all southward.

At (687 219) are the remains of the Roman signal station, remains in two senses, for not only is the site much reduced in height — the central tower could well have been 100 feet high — it is reduced in area, some of it having slid 360 feet on to the beach. Originally the site was protected by a V–ditch, 28 feet wide and 6 feet deep with an inner wall, and the central tower was 50 feet square. Uncovered in a well were the bodies of 14 adults and children, almost certainly the garrison and their families, slaughtered and thrown into the well when the station was over–run at the end of the fourth century. It was a sad fate, but do not become too sombre as the cliff–edge walk here is magnificent. Note that occasionally the edge fence has disappeared — be

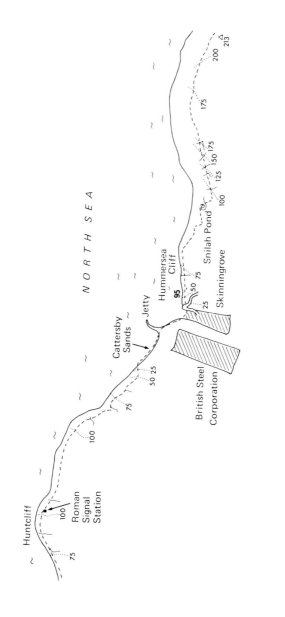

careful: if you get too close you may go with the next fall.

At (692 217) an old railway is reached and followed for a short while. The railway was coming from Skinningrove, the difficult–to–avoid works complex on the skyline being what was once the Skinningrove Iron Works. The path, a little away from the cliff edge after it leaves the old railway, heads for re–claimed spoil tips but drops down an obvious valley before them to reach a cliff–base path that is followed to Skinningrove jetty. There the village comes into view, an array of terraced houses and pigeon lofts. It is hardly the highlight of the walk, but it is a link with much of the industrial waste we have passed on the Moors. So, rather than criticise, let us look at the history of the area's ironstone industry.

The history is a very long one, an Iron Age bloomery dating to 550 BC having been found on Lewisham Moor. By the early Middle Ages there were a couple of hundred such bloomeries — the technology had changed little in the 1700 years since Levisham — dotted all over the Moors, their operation being chiefly in the hands of the large monastic houses. Peter de Brus gave the Prior of Guisborough rights to search Glaisdale and Eskdale for iron ore in the thirteenth century, though production was chiefly in the hands of the Cistercian houses of Rievaulx and Bilsdale.

The source of ironstone, the local ore, for the bloomeries, was the bell pit, a vertical shaft dug into the seam, from the bottom of which the miners dug outward in all directions, creating a bell shape. It was dangerous work — the undermined roof could collapse and great skill was needed to know when to abandon one pit in favour of another. The bloomery itself used a mixture of ore, lime and charcoal in a stove box, a primitive blast being supplied by bellows and shaped wooden draught–boards. The iron was never really molten, needing constant hammering to get rid of impurities, and it took many days to produce a lump of iron. In time the bloomeries denuded the local wood, 16 tons of timber being needed for every ton of iron and the clearance being accelerated by the arrival of the blast furnace.

Eventually coal took over from wood as the fuel source for

Huntcliff from Saltburn sands

iron–making. With no coal reserves, this could have been the end of the local industry had it not been for the discovery of the true extent of local ironstone seams. The story is told that someone walking on the Easton Hills stubbed his toe on an ironstone nodule and the industry was re–born. It all sounds a little too pat, though a continuation of the story shows more realistic behaviour. The nodules were sent by ship to Tyneside, but the collectors sometimes supplemented their finds with the odd brownish pebble, so much so that eventually the Tyneside ironmasters sent Joseph Beswick to the area to find the real seams for them to exploit. He found the Kettleness seams but his employers were unimpressed, seeing only the difficulties of transporting the ore. Eventually, however, the Grosmont seams were uncovered and exploitation began in earnest. Later Kettleness was mined, as were Skinningrove (where the price asked by the landowner for permission to dig was, reputedly, one glass of good brandy) and, most famously of all, Rosedale.

By 1856 annual production had broken the 1 million ton barrier, with the bulk being shifted by rail now rather than by ship. Rail transport was not without hazards: a section of land collapsing into a mine near Guisborough one day left the line, still intact, 40 feet above the new hole. Fortunately a ganger stopped the approaching train. The mines themselves were surprisingly safe, being relatively gas–free, which also allowed carbide lights to be used by the miners. There were problems, however; the seams were narrow and variable and near Skelton one shaft sunk through the sandstone struck an underground lake, which dumped 15 tons of water per minute into the mine.

By 1873 there were 40 mines and in 1883 these produced 6¾ million tons of ore, the highest-ever production rate. But the business was always on a knife–edge, and by 1920 production had fallen back to 1 million tons, though the decline had been slowed by the 1914–18 War. The 1939–45 War improved trade, but the end was in sight. In 1964 the Skelton mine closed, a closure that seems likely to be final. In its history the Moors' ironstone industry is estimated to have produced 350 million tons.

Most of the ironstone was taken out of the area, to Middlesbrough and beyond, for iron–making. Indeed, the

Cleveland iron industry has a fine place in the history of iron–
making, employing at one stage Percy Gilchrist who, with his
cousin Sidney Gilchrist Thomas, revolutionised the process of
steel–making by inventing a way of preparing steel from high
phosphorus ores. Within the area covered by our walk there were
few ironworks. One was opened at Whitby, the Whitby Iron
Company, but it was not a success. It made its first iron in June
1860 but was up for sale in early 1861. There were no buyers. The
owners tried again in 1862, and closed the works as a complete
failure in 1864.

Here at Skinningrove there was more success, the ironworks
surviving, though not on local ore, up to the present. The original
owner, a Quaker, Joseph Pease, built the village with a school
and chapel but with no pub. Today the works are owned by the
British Steel Company and make special profiles, a collective term
for volume production of intricate shapes, such as bulldozer
tracks. I have to admit I do not really know how they do the
work, but one thing is certain: whatever they do they need a vast
amount of room to do it.

Skinningrove was not always full of ironworkers. In the early
nineteenth century there was a tiny fishing village here, men
from which netted a merman one day that was kept captive in the
village. He ate raw fish and tolerated visitors, though he never
spoke, just screeching occasionally. Eventually he escaped, swam
out to sea, turned and waved goodbye, and disappeared. Sadly,
no one thought to write a description of the creature, whatever it
was.

When the American privateer Paul Jones came this way he
shelled the village, though it was to the south that he really had
to fight, as we shall see. Later, during the 1914–18 War the village
was bombed by Zeppelins, apparently in mistake for Teeside!

Beyond the jetty, the beck on which Skinningrove was built is
crossed to a road running seaward (north). Follow this road
upward around a steep right–hand bend immediately beyond
which, at (715 201), a stile left allows the cliff edge to be regained.
This is Hummersea Cliff, on top of which is a pillbox, a relic from

the 1939–45 war, when the little inlet of Skinningrove was
defended against sea–borne invasion rather than air attack.

At (728 198) the route goes right (south–east) around Snilah
Pond, a nasty–looking, effluent–polluted stretch of water not at
all in keeping with the nature of the cliff edge here. After a few
yards, at (729 197), the Way turns left (east) again, passing
Warren Farm before crossing fields on the climb to the top of
Boulby Cliffs. This is quite a climb, the top of the cliff being 660
feet above sea-level. The cliffs are often quoted as the highest in
England, which they are not, a couple of Devon's cliffs
overtopping them by 300 feet, but Boulby does have the highest
cliffs on the east coast of England.

The name Boulby is said to derive from Boll's Farm, but there is
also a legend that the burial mound of Beowulf was on the clifftop
here (the saga–hero wanted to be buried at the highest point of
the north–east coast), though no site is obvious. Such
disturbances as are obvious are associated with ironstone mining
to feed the Skinningrove works, and alum mining. Inland, a little
from the route, is the Cleveland Potash Ltd. mine that continues
this history of extracting minerals at Boulby. The potash deposits,
salts deposited in a desert lagoon some 200 million years ago, lie
nearly 5000 feet below the visible mining buildings. The mine
came into full operation as late as 1974 and was, therefore, built
within the boundaries of an existing National Park. When the
idea was mooted it caused some understandable dissent and
concern. The buildings have been blended reasonably well, but
clearly they are an intrusion. Perhaps we should be happy the
situation is not worse, though the ease and frequency with which
governments decide that projects such as this one are unique,
and therefore cannot create a precedent, bothers me
considerably. A unique mine here, a unique road there, and the
National Park is much reduced.

It is a long, and not easily accomplished journey to the foot of
the cliffs, but those who do make it are treated to a feast of
geology, the tall cliffs offering a considerable slice through the
Jurassic rock sequence.

The headland, because of its height, is also a fine vantage
point: the views south–east along the Cleveland Way to Staithes

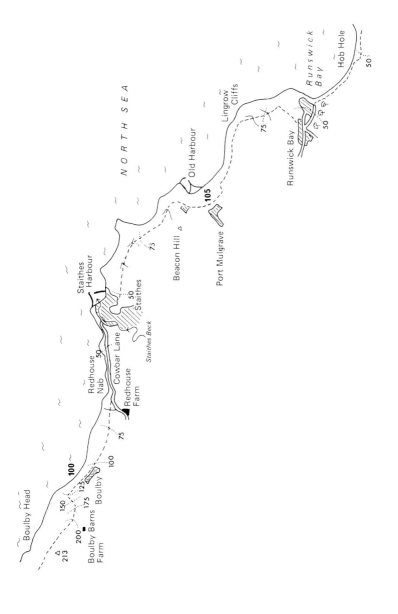

N O R T H   S E A

Boulby Head

△ 213

Boulby Barns Farm

200

175

150

100

125

Boulby

100

Redhouse Nab

75

Redhouse Farm

Cowbar Lane

50

Staithes Beck

Staithes

50

Staithes Harbour

Beacon Hill △

75

105

Old Harbour

Port Mulgrave

Lingrow Cliffs

75

R u n s w i c k   B a y

Hob Hole

50

Runswick Bay

50

50

and on towards Whitby, and back towards Saltburn are excellent. This spot is wonderful in winter, with the sea battering the cliff base. It certainly can make you glad you do not live here!

The route forward is obvious because of the extensive view. Stay on the cliff side of the field boundaries until you are level with Boulby Barns Farm (753 191) where the path leads due east to meet a sea–going wall (756 193). Go along the wall and follow it around right (south–east) to the little hamlet of Boulby itself.

Follow a lane through the hamlet to (765 188) where a path goes east across fields to the road at (770 187). Cowbar Lane, named, perhaps, from 'coalburn' for a beacon fire to warn smugglers of the approach of the Preventative Officers, is followed into Staithes.

Staithes

By entering the village along Cowbar Lane, the bridge over
Staithes Beck is crossed, one of the most photographed bridges in
one of the most photographed villages. Normally the backdrop to
the bridge is the exposed rock strata of Cowbar Nab, the sheer,
loose cliff being the reason why the village is squeezed on to the
south side of the beck and why, as a result, the cottages face
north, and the winter's cold northerlies. Small wonder Staithes
breeds a hardy folk. And as if thoughts of those cutting winds
were not enough to chill the blood, be careful on the bridge: you
may meet the ghost of a young girl decapitated by a rock falling
from Cowbar Nab.

Staithes has been called the Clovelly of the North, but that does
not seem a particulary apt description: the enclosed, sun–less
street here can appear dour in comparison to the more
seductively positioned Devon village, though each has an
atmosphere that is strangely compelling. Dog Laup is said to be
the narrowest passage in the North of England, a suggestion that
is more likely to be accurate than the name, Captain Cook, of a
cottage near it. Cook was here, as we have seen, but his old
quarters slipped into the sea long ago. Even if it were not for the
easily eroded boulder clay, the loss of the village into the sea was
inevitable. Two tired mermaids came ashore here many years
ago, exhausted from fighting against the stormy sea. They were
held captive and exhibited but escaped when, after many
months, the villagers relaxed their guard. As they swam away,
one turned and cursed Staithes, crying that the sea would flow to
Jackdaw's Well, and so it has.

When the Domesday survey was made the village here was
Scetune, a name that survives as Seaton further inland. Probably
at that time the coast was continuously threatened by North Sea
raiders, and an inland site was preferred. Seaton Hall Farm was
the old church site, and three stone coffins have been discovered
there: one was recognised as such only after it had served time as
a cattle trough! In the fifteenth century, when things quietened,

the village moved down the beck, though no one can explain why
the new name appeared, or why the local pronunciation is
'Steers'.

From the time the village moved to the sea the chief trade was
fishing, although Cowbar Nab did offer some mining: ironstone,
alum and a little jet. One mid–nineteenth–century writer
described the village menfolk in their 'blue Guernsey and
sou'westers, with lobster pots, or yellow from head to foot with
thick dust'. The Guernseys were knitted by the wives, perhaps
wearing their now–famous bonnets, when they were not
repairing net or preparing bait or helping to launch the boats.
And, as if all that was not enough, if the catch was consistently
bad the women assembled at midnight, killed a pigeon, removed
its heart, stuck it full of pins and burned it over a charcoal fire, a
rite guaranteed to bring the witch who had bewitched the boats
to the house door to bargain. What a remarkable procedure! And
what happened, I wonder, if no one came? But someone, at some
time, must have come: such rituals cannot carry on indefinitely in
the continuous absence of a witch.

The boat the men used was the coble, and, apart from their
engines, the ones that lie in the beck would be recognised by
Captain Cook: sharp, steep bows, broad in the middle and a stern
cut square for beck launching, or pointed for beach launching, to
ease the burden of rowing back on shore. The fish were herring
from July to September, cod and turbot for the rest of the year.
Staithes, in the last quarter of the nineteenth century, was
recognised as the best herring port with the best herring waters in
Britain. At that time there were 400 men at work on the boats,
then sail–driven. The large steam boats from the big ports killed
the trade, but there has recently been a slight upswing, with local
boats taking salmon and lobster. As if to capture the old and the
new, an inn we pass is the Cod and Lobster.

As in all the North Sea ports, the press–gang operated in
Staithes from time to time, the earliest record here being the
taking of 16 men in 1593, a tragedy for the wives and children left

Staithes

to fend for themselves. Pressed men from Staithes served at Trafalgar, and some spent many years in French prisoner-of-war camps. One man was actually taken from his boat and did not see his unborn daughter until she was 14, by which time his wife had become rich and owned several local cottages.

As elsewhere on the coast, there were smugglers here, with the usual clutch of tales about secret passages. One pleasing story concerns a smuggler who hung a bag of gold coins out of a window when the Preventative Officer came, and when the man had gone found that the bag had gone too — out with the tide! If you are inclined to disbelieve that story, just see how close the houses are to the high tides. The bowsprit of a boat once went through a window of the Cod and Lobster. I do not know if there was insurance in those days, but if so the claim form must have come as a surprise to the insurer's clerk.

On a much sadder note, a local narrative poem tells of the night in 1888 when the lifeboat shepherded 43 of 44 cobles to safety in an appalling storm, returning with an exhausted crew to search for the last. The lifeboat did not return but two men were washed ashore, a dead lifeboatman and the live crewman of the last coble. The worst was feared but the lifeboat, with the rest of the crew, was washed, rudderless and helpless, into the Tees. It had capsized but self-righted, with the sad loss of one crewman.

We leave Staithes by passing the Cod and Lobster and turning right (south) up Church Street. The church, as if anyone would not have guessed, is dedicated to St. Peter.

I am always sad at leaving Staithes. It is a quirky little port with an undeniable charm and I always decide to return. I do wish I had been here on a festival sport's day in 1797 when the big event was 'To wit, a fish skin purse containing SILVER will be run or rolled for in sacks, a man and a boy in each sack'. I am not sure which intrigues me the most, the race or the prize.

Lingrow and Kettleness from Port Mulgrave

At the top of the lane fork left on a track that leads easily across fields, one field away from the cliff edge at first, but reaching it again at (792 184). The cliff edge is then followed into the village of Port Mulgrave. The port itself is down at the cliff base and cannot be reached except by an energetic scramble. But there is little to see: even from the clifftop the erosion of the old harbour is obvious. The port was constructed solely for the local mines, and when they closed, it closed too. It had been fed in fine style, by a narrow-gauge railway that tunnelled its way from the mines directly to the base of the cliff.

The name, still given to the small collection of houses the Way passes, was borrowed from inland here and, more famously, a little way south, where the Mulgrave Woods are well worth visiting. They contain one complete castle, a nineteenth–century mock–Gothic building, and the remains of two others — one only earth banks now, from the eleventh century, and one more complete, from the early thirteenth. It is too far to deviate from the Cleveland Way, but go in spring to see the snowdrops and primroses.

Beyond Port Mulgrave the Way stays at the cliff edge, with an expanding view of beautiful Runswick Bay ahead. At (809 165) the path goes sharp right (south-west) in order to reach Runswick village. The turn is near two small ponds, usually more noticeable for their irises and reeds than for their water. If you miss the turn, don't panic: the cliff path also reaches the village, though in less straightforward fashion.

Runswick Bay

Runswick is a prettier village than Staithes; pretty, that is, in the postcard or calendar sense. It has more neatly laid out cottages, each with a little garden, each white–washed below its red pantiles. It is, of course, built on flatter land, and has the distinct advantage of being sheltered from the northerly winds by the bulk of Lingrow Knowle. Not that the shelter has always saved it. In 1682 most of the village slid down on to the beach during a storm that undermined the cliff. Strangely, 150 years later, the village at the other end of the bay did the same thing.

In winter the number of the pretty cottages that are occupied is seen to be very small. Runswick suffers from the holiday home, the wasting disease of villages and one they find difficult to cure, as rising cottage prices and falling numbers of local jobs cause increasing numbers of young people to leave. In the sense that this leaves us with unspoilt villages, the trend is a blessing, but for the few 'real' villagers left, the loss of community is a tragedy; for the rest of us the loss of a way of life is one more extinction.

That is all very sobering as we drop down an extraordinary steep section of new road to a car-park and then down on to the beach, the more so when remembering a story from March 1901, when the men of the village were caught by a ferocious storm while out fishing. Since it was they who manned the lifeboat, no help for them was possible until the women of the village and the older men launched the lifeboat themselves, no mean feat with a heavy boat that needed to be pushed beyond the surf to loosen it from its cradle. What a people they must have been that lived here. As a memorial, the women received a dinner and plaque in Manchester, a nice gesture, but probably little to compare with the sense of unity the village must have felt at the time.

On the beach it is immediately obvious to those with a keen sense of geology that Runswick Bay poses a classic examination question. At our end of the beach, the west end, there is sand, while at the other end, where we are going, there is bare rock. Why is this? Discuss.

At the point on the beach where the second beck cuts through the cliff are the Hob Holes, in part natural caves, in part the remains of old jet workings, now seriously eroded by the sea. Here lived a hob, a goblin, who could cure whooping cough in children, if he was asked properly —

Hob Hole Hob
My bairn's gotten t'kink-cough
Tak't off, tak't off

At (816 153), a couple of hundred yards past the yacht clubhouse, follow the beck south and climb up to the clifftop. This is Claymoor End, the name seeming very appropriate in wet weather, when care is needed with footings. At the clifftop continue east along the edge and into Kettleness.

It was on a stormy December night in 1829 that Kettleness slipped into the sea. It had rained so long and so hard that the boulder clay on which the village stood had become liquid mud, as too had some of the cliff behind the village. Suddenly, though quietly and slowly, the whole lot started to slide towards the sea — cliff, houses and people. So slowly did it happen that the villagers were able to escape their homes, though they had nowhere to go because, as a contemporary account has it, 'the sinking cliff pressed on them behind, the yawning deep threatened before them'. It seems likely that the villagers would have been wiped out, literally, but there was a ship, the alum carrier *Henry*, offshore, and it was able to take them all off.

As well as the village the alum mines also disappeared, not to be re–opened until 1831. At several points along the route we have passed the remains of alum mines, but at no point has the industry left such a mark as here at Kettleness, so it seems an appropriate place to ask — what is alum?

It is a complex mineral, a mixture of the sulphates of aluminium, potassium and ammonia, that was and still is, though to a lesser extent, used in the textile industry to fix dyes, and in tanning. Several centuries ago it was also used in the manufacture of parchment and candles.

In the late sixteenth century the Pope had a virtual monopoly

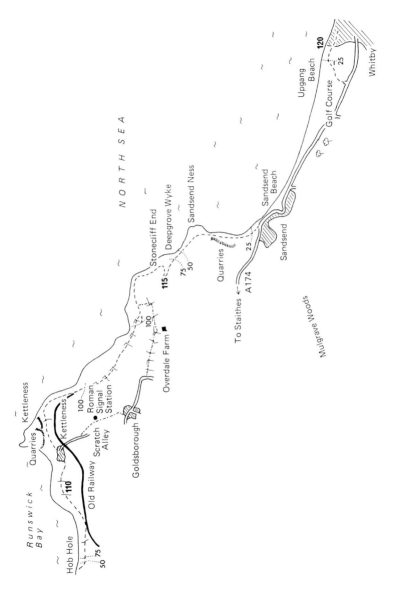

of alum production in Europe, based on mines near Rome, and the industry was an important source of revenue. Sir Thomas Challoner, squire of Guisborough, was on a visit to the Holy See when he noticed that near the Pope's Puteoli mines the leaves on the trees were tinged with the same colour as they were on his own estate, and that the soil was also similar, a whitish clay that sparkled at night and would never freeze. Realising that if his suspicions that the soils were the same were correct, then he could challenge the Papal monopoly (and make the odd shilling or two for himself), Challoner looked about for someone who could tell him how to extract the mineral. He therefore bribed a couple of Italian workers to go back with him to Yorkshire. So important was the monopoly that the See guarded its workers, and the men had to be smuggled out of Italy in empty sherry casks. When the Holy See realised what had happened, the Pope anathematised Sir Thomas and his accomplices: 'May they be cursed in the hair of their head, and in their brain, cheeks, groin, veins, genitals, bowels, and in all the interior parts of their bodies to the very stomach . . .' And, as if that were not enough: 'May they be cursed in all their joints from the top of their head to the soles of their feet, nor may there be any soundness left in them.' As a nineteenth–century writer noted, 'the infallibility [of the Pope] is, in this respect, to be doubted' as none of the curses 'denounced by his Holiness, have fallen upon this heretic'.

What a remarkable story. It may be worth adding the suggestion that there are those who do not believe a word of it, and claim that Challoner obtained workers and techniques quite legitimately from France!

Whatever the truth, Challoner certainly did open the first alum mine in England, at a remarkable saving to the Exchequer. Quick to take advantage, the Stuart kings created their own monopoly, effectively charging landowners huge rents on their own land, a situation which survived for some time.

There were mines all over the area crossed by the Cleveland Way, the biggest being at Boulby, on the site now occupied by the

Runswick

potash mine. It is at Kettleness and at Sandsend, however, that the greatest effect of the operations can be seen. The alum is obtained from 'alum shale', a rock found in the Upper Liassic series of Yorkshire's Jurassic rocks. The extraction of usable mineral is as remarkable a story as that of Challoner's founding of the industry, and a quick resume of the relevant stages is entertaining.

Over 100 tons of shale were needed to produce 1 ton of alum, the process starting with calcining of the shale, a slow roasting over a wood fire. The calcining heap could be 100 feet high and would burn and stink for up to nine months. The roasted shale was then steeped in water, with just the right density necessary to ensure that the mineral salts went into solution: the classic test was that an egg would just float in the correct mixture. The solution was then boiled in huge pans; there were 80 at Boulby, producing a fearful mixture of smoke and steam. The concentrated liquid was then poured into tanks, and potash and ammonia were added. At this point what was a disagreeable process became breathtakingly unpleasant.

Potash was obtained from the ash of burning seaweed, huge quantities being brought in, fired and raked as it burnt. The smell was indescribable. But worse was to come. Ammonia was obtained from urine, and since animals could not be persuaded to provide it in reasonable containers, human urine was used. There are records of a penny per gallon being paid in Guisborough but the chief source was London, where collecting barrels were set up on street corners. This pleased local publicans and their clientele but, not surprisingly, it pleased the local householders not at all. Five pence per barrel was paid to collectors, and it cost three–farthings per barrel to ship it to Yorkshire. We read, 'the small vessels engaged in this trade bore an unsavoury name [only the name?], and no stronger word of contempt could be levelled at a mariner than to say he was the captain of such a ship'.

So, with the burnt seaweed and the urine added, the mixture was stewed for a few days, until the alum crystallised. These first

Runswick Bay

crystals were re–dissolved in clean water, a second crystallisation producing pure alum.

At Kettleness hundreds of men laboured for decades in this unpleasant industry. In the course of their labours they reduced the cliff to half its original height, creating a wilderness that is still dangerous from their efforts and those of the shaft–boring ironstone workers, who gave up in disgust, not at the smell, but at the thin, variable seams. The cliff is still rugged, still strangely beautiful, but it is certainly no monument to man's involvement with nature, except in a savage sense. Our only compensation is that the delightful stone cottages and houses in local towns and villages were raised by profits from the cliff's destruction.

All along the coast to Scarborough there were signal stations set up by the Romans to warn of invaders from the east. We have passed one at Saltburn, but another can be seen by taking a slight detour along the road from Kettleness to Goldsborough. At (832 153) a path, Scratch Alley, leads to it at (835 152).

The station itself, a 47–foot–square tower which was probably 90 feet high with walls 5-foot thick, was defended by a ditch 12 feet across and 4 feet deep, further protected by a tall, 4–foot thick wall. In a corner of the site the skeletons of men and a dog were found, their unburied bodies evidence of a violent end.

Even now this cliff is used to scan the sea. Beyond Kettleness village the Cleveland Way follows a track to the coastguard station and lookout: the view back to Runswick Bay is excellent. From here the shape is half-moon, but to a sailing-ship captain, drawn into the Bay by the wind and unable, because of it, to clear the points of Lingrow or Kettleness depending upon his direction of travel, the Bay was sickle–shaped, the points slicing open the bottom of his ship. There is an elemental, other–worldliness about this spot, and it is not surprising to find that the far–off pounding of waves on rock here was once thought by some at Runswick to be the noise of fairies beating their clothes as they

Kettleness

washed them in the Kettleness springs.

At (838 154) the path reaches the track of the old Middlesbrough–to–Whitby railway, near where it entered a short tunnel. This tunnel and the second, longer one are dangerous. They have been blocked, but if ever they can be, they should not be entered. The second tunnel starts at (841 150), the path keeping to the cliff edge. At Stonecliff End (855 142) the Wayfarer goes over a stile and turns right (west). Shortly after, look for steps to the left that are followed to the exit from the second tunnel (854 142). It is sad, in one sense, that the railway no longer exists, it must have been a very dramatic trip, emerging from the darkness of the tunnel to this view southward. The Way now follows the old railway track into Sandsend.

As the track is followed, the Wayfarer threads a way through the Sandsend alum industry, passing, to the right, the remains of several old quarries and spoil heaps — one of the latter forming Asylum Hill — and, to the left, some sandstone blocks that are all that remain of one part of the works. It is very interesting to note the extent to which nature has re–colonised the quarries in the century since production stopped. A booklet produced by the National Park Office describes the walk along the track and the plant and wildlife that can be seen, and is well worth the small cost asked.

Sandsend is an amalgam of two villages, one standing on Sandsend Beck, the other on East Rock Beck. Once it flourished, with alum and jet workings on Sandsend Ness, and the railway bringing people and prosperity. There was a hotel on the cliff edge, famous as a smugglers' haunt, the cliff below riddled with contraband–filled caves. Now it is just a winter–quiet, summer–busy seaside resort, at one end of the best stretch of sand along our coastal walk. This is the place for castle–building and paddling, for sand between your toes, and in your egg–and–tomato sandwiches.

Inland from here are the Mulgrave castles and Lythe village, but Sandsend beach is the great draw and it is possible, if the tide

Whitby from Sandsend

is right, to walk into Whitby along it. But do be careful not to be caught awkwardly by the rising tide, particularly at the Whitby end. The 'cliffs' here are the remains of the 200–foot–thick Ice Age debris, the boulder clay, which is as unstable a medium as ever Nature produced.

If the tide is in, the Wayfarer has to retreat to the A174 that, at first, runs at the beach edge but later errs on the side of caution and runs inland. At (879 117) a lane left (north) beyond the golf course is taken, back to the cliff edge. Here we go eastward along the path at the edge, into Whitby.

Whitby

The Way eventually joins Westcliff Walk along the clifftop near Whitby's North Promenade, arriving at the end where the sea cliffs and the River Esk cliffs meet. Here, with a view forward to the Abbey and the church across the Esk, and down to the harbour walls, stands Captain Cook, surveying the old town from which he made his first sea voyage. Beyond the statue, framing parts of the old town as we approach, are the jawbones of a whale.

In 1753 two Whitby boats, the *Henry and Mary* and the *Sea Nymph* went north to catch whales. Within 20 years there were more than a dozen boats, and though the total was never more than 20, Whitby became the greatest whaling port on the coast, bigger even than Hull. It was a hard life; lime juice for the prevention of scurvy was not compulsory on non–Royal Navy ships until 1854, and even after that it was not universally used. In 1866 a Hull whaler was trapped in Arctic pack ice and the whole crew died, painfully, of the condition. Those that did not die often returned ill and starving from a trip where the cold and the dangers of hand–held harpoons were killers in themselves.

Whitby abandoned whaling in 1837, having lived on the profits of almost 3000 whales, innumerable seal, walrus, polar bear, and, apparently, 41 unicorns — were these narwhals? — profits which maintained as many as half of the town's population. The whales produced oil for lamps and bone for corsets but the trade died when coal–gas replaced oil and fashions changed. The last English whaling boat was wrecked in the Humber in 1869, although Scottish boats continued for a short time after.

It has become fashionable to lyricise the ancient crafts today, even occasionally to the extent of putting on pedestals folk like the Whitby whalers, whose trade is seen somehow as noble, the pursuit of a large, possibly aggressive quarry in its own environment with a minimum of technology. The reality appears to be that the trade was brutal and bloody, with the competition to be chief whaler as nasty a race between greedy men as could be envisaged. The jaws on Westcliff came, in 1963, from an 82–foot whale, weighing over 100 tons, a true monarch of the sea. I am willing to wager that the bones looked better on the whale than they do here.

By contrast, Whitby jet is almost certainly worth extracting from the cliffs, few people finding it unpleasant to see or touch, despite its dark associations of being a funereal gem. Jet is an oddity, not being a mineral at all but the compressed remains, the fossil, if you prefer, of trees that grew perhaps 200 million years ago. It is, therefore, a type of anthracite, though it is much harder than any other coal. It is so hard that it will take being machined, a quality that together with its woody texture makes it ideal for jewellery. As jewellery, it has been found in local Bronze Age round barrows, still as a basic beach pebble though in some cases worked by a flint knapper. One necklace contains 600 pieces; pendants, rings and buttons have also been found. Jet clearly formed a part of Bronze Age trade, pieces having been found as far away as Ireland.

The Romans knew of it — Solinus writing in AD 80 mentions that it occurs in abundance in parts of Britain — and the Saxons also prized it. In AD 670 Caedmon, the poet from the Abbey whom we shall meet again, even noted a curious property of jet —

'Tis black and shiny, smooth and ever light
'Twill draw up straws, if rubbed 'till hot and bright

Caedmon was noticing electrostatic charge and pre-dating by 13 centuries a General Science demonstration that I once watched, fascinated.

The Saxons used jet in Whitby Abbey, and pebbles found on the beach continued to be prized until the early nineteenth–century discovery of machining gave the trade a further boost. Later, Queen Victoria's interest in jet jewellery during her long mourning for Prince Albert gave jet working fresh impetus and it became the major Whitby industry. At first, need was satisfied by beachcombing, but later the cliffs were mined, and later still more mines were opened in many places on the coast and on the

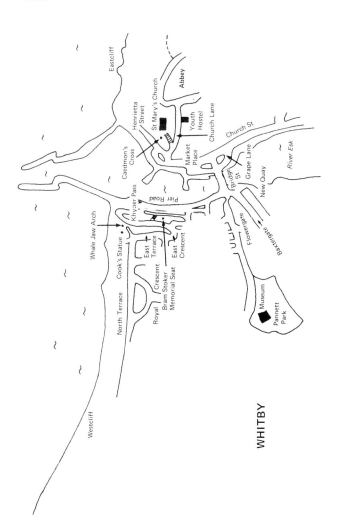

WHITBY

Moors' escarpment. By the last quarter of the last century the boom was over, although there has been continuing interest and a small–scale jewellery production ever since.

One of the most fascinating aspects of jet is that it has been seen as a patent medicine throughout history. The Romans burnt it, believing the inhaled smoke cured hysteria, and they powdered it in wine to cure toothache. In the Middle Ages, if dissolved in water, jet was believed to 'cure' an adder bite, and a French text notes that its smoke, inhaled, would relieve the female womb.

The early history of Whitby is the history of the Abbey we shall pass on our Way south–east. The first Abbey was Saxon, and the town name derives from this period when, at first, it was interchangeable with Prestby, the priest's farm. The natural harbour of the Esk inlet led to a rapid expansion of the fishing trade: Leland, the Elizabethan traveller, mentions Whitby — 'a great fischer towne'. It was also, at the time, a place of dubious law. In July 1526 French pirates brought in and auctioned a ship and its cargo that they had taken in the Humber. Even the Abbot bought a few items, and was hauled before the Star Chamber when the true owner turned up, understandably miffed. Two centuries later a townsman, John Stephenson, was executed as a pirate, having served with the famous Bartholomew Roberts. Stephenson may not have been entirely blameworthy, though history does not record all the facts: Whitby was the local headquarters of the press–gang, and a few pressed men finished up as pirates when their original ships were taken by privateers.

At a later stage the town added shipbuilding to its industries, a trade that seemed to require an inordinate amount of refreshment. There were ramming pots (of ale) drunk after the keel had been laid and the stem and stern posts raised. There was the blacking drink when caulking started, and several others at interim points. Finally, when the boat was finished, the oldest apprentice shipwright had to kiss the first lady who passed — after the reaming pot had been drunk, of course.

Later still there was an effort to set up a Whitby spa, using the waters of a mineral spring at the base of West Cliff. It was not a great success.

From where we stand, near the whale's jawbones, we are above a small beach on the west bank of the River Esk, a beach where Lewis Carroll reputedly wrote parts of *Alice in Wonderland*. To our right (south) is a memorial seat to another famous book with more obviously Whitby associations.

It is also the start of a very interesting walk around the town, for which a leaflet can be obtained at the Tourist Information Office at New Quay. On our way to the seat consider a local story, and a local saying: 'happy is the corpse that the rain rains on', an allusion to an ancient tradition. The story tells of the burial of fishermen at St. Mary's Church. On the night following an interment, six jet–black horses pulled a coach up the hill to the church, accompanied by two black–robed outriders carrying torches from which sparks flew. At the church ghostly mourners climbed out of the coach, to be joined inside by the dead man, who climbed out of the fresh grave for the occasion. At midnight all of them climbed back into the coach, that was driven then at high speed over the cliff.

The memorial seat, at the south end of Spion Kop, is to Bram Stoker, author of *Dracula*, one early part of which is set in Whitby. On the night of a dramatic but oddly sudden storm, the Russian schooner *Demeter* is driven onto the eastern pier and then into the harbour. All the crew are gone except the captain, who lies dead, but all this is not known until after a huge dog, Dracula in disguise, has leapt ashore and disappeared into the night. The Count spends some of his time in Whitby in the grave of a suicide in St. Mary's churchyard, before moving to London in a crate of earth imported by a lawyer living at No 7 The Crescent, now East Crescent, above and behind the memorial seat.

I find the use of this real town, with recognisable features — even if the grave cannot be located in the churchyard — fascinating, adding interest both to the book and the port. It is, however, hardly worth reading the book just for the Whitby chapters. It is a long and occasionally long–winded book, but far more subtle than any of the spin–off cinema epics.

To reach the seat we have descended the Khyber Pass — that really is the name! — that hairpins its way down to the west side of the river. The road was cut in 1848 when the last major

development of the west side was undertaken. The east side is all
older, though Baxtergate here dates, in part, to the early fifteenth
century and Flowergate is mentioned, as the manor of Flare, in
the Domesday Book. Also on the west side is the town museum
in Pannett Park, a most interesting site, one room of which is
devoted to Whitby sailors, Captain Cook and the William
Scoresbys, father and son. The elder Scoresby was the best
whaling captain of his era, inventor of the crow's nest, and still
the holder of the record for closest approach to the North Pole in
a sailing ship, at 500 miles. The younger William was a whaler
when young but was also a scientist whose survey of the East
Greenland coast and 1820 book of Arctic observations are
acceptably correct. He was later ordained as a Church of England
clergyman.

There are, in fact, a number of interesting streets and houses
on the Esk's west banks, the town fathers having made a
reasonable job of steering the difficult course between dead–but–
interesting old port, and commercially successful but space–
invader–ridden holiday resort. On the eastern bank of the river
the task has been easier, the town being smaller, with less land
available for development.

To reach the east bank, Whitby's famous bridge has to be
crossed. The current bridge swings, and is from the early part of
this century. It had a long line of ancestors, however, a bridge
being mentioned in 1351. The best, visually at least, must have
been the spindly double drawbridge that spanned the river from
1766 to 1835 and kept getting caught up in ships' rigging. The
present bridge not only links the east and west banks, but
separates the upper and lower harbours, swinging for a few
hours only around high water to allow transfers. The harbour
covers 80 acres, the port still being a major local industry,
exporting grain and still importing all manner of goods, and
servicing the local fishing fleet.

Whitby East Side is a wonderful little place, full of interesting
nooks and crannies and with an enviably long history. Church

Whitby

Street was called Kirkgate in 1318, and ends in the old Market
Square, still a lively spot. Sandgate dates from 1401, while Grape
Lane — the name derives from 'Grope', because it was so narrow
and dark — contains the house where Captain Cook stayed,
slinging his hammock in the attic.

At the south end of Church Street, an odd ceremony takes
place each Ascension Eve in the old harbour. The story goes that
hunters out in Eskdale in ancient times wounded a boar that
stumbled into a hermit's hut and died. A squabble followed, the
hunters wanting their quarry, the hermit wanting to maintain the
sanctity of his cell, and during the skirmish the hermit fell,
wounded. The hunters fled to Scarborough, from where they
were brought back by the Abbot of Whitby to face the dying
hermit. Without the old man's forgiveness they would be
executed, but he granted it to them, on the condition that at
9 a.m. on Ascension Eve they should construct, in the harbour
mud, a hedge that would withstand three tides when the builders
shouted 'out on you' at the first receding tide.

So, if you join the several hundred others early on that day
near the old harbour, you will see three men in boots on the
harbour floor. Two men build a short length of hazel hedge,
weaving yethers between the upright stowers; when they have
finished, the third man blows a horn and shouts at the water. The
ceremony is known as the Penny Hedge, supposedly because the
hermit specified that the hedge had to be cut and trimmed with a
penny knife, though it is much more likely that the word derives
from penance.

History records no knights or abbot of the names given in the
story, belying an enjoyable tale. But the ceremony must have
some basis. One clue is an alternative name, horngarth, deriving
from horn (cattle) and garth (hedge). Probably it relates to a tax
imposed on locals by the Abbot of Whitby, paid by the erection or
maintenance of cattle fencing, or by the boundary marking of the
Abbey's land.

Near the other end of Church Street, next to the Market, is the
Fish Pier where the Whitby lifeboat is housed. The Whitby boat,
though not the one now housed here, is famous as the one
launched after an epic moorland haul in 1881. A ship was in

difficulties in a blizzard in Robin Hood's Bay and the Whitby boat, which could not be launched at the town because of mountainous seas, was hauled 6 miles through snowdrifts by teams of horses supplied by local farmers, with men breaking trail and women holding lights. The boat was launched in the freezing waters, losing seven oars smashed to splinters by the waves, but it managed to disembark the ship's crew. But if that rescue is a monument to the lifeboatmen's tradition of success, the penalties of failure were displayed in 9 February 1861 when the Whitby boat capsized only yards from shore while going to the rescue of a schooner that had run aground. In full view of hundreds of onlookers, 12 men of the 13-man crew drowned, the only survivor being the man wearing the new–fangled cork life–jacket. The tragedy left 10 widows and 44 fatherless children, an aftermath as appalling as can be contemplated but made worse by repercussions from a chance remark made at the inquest by the survivor, Henry Freeman. He noted that the men had taken a couple of tots of rum — tragedy struck on what would have been the sixth rescue of the day. Hearing this, a local temperance man suggested that alcohol was, in part, responsible for the tragedy. He was promptly burned in effigy on West Cliff and was lucky that it was only the effigy.

   At the end of Church Street is Henrietta Street, once called Haggerlythe and holding a battery that tried to engage the privateer Paul Jones when he entered the harbour. Sadly, the battery canon exploded, killing the two men manning it. The road here was several times destroyed by land–slippage from the unstable cliff above. Some land–slips brought down coffins from the churchyard. Did Bram Stoker know this?

   From Henrietta Street go up Church Lane and take the 199 Church Steps to the Abbey Plain that holds St. Mary's Church and the Abbey ruins in one of the most dramatic positions in Britain, let alone Yorkshire.

   St. Mary's, said Pevsner, was 'one of the churches one is fondest of in all England'. Inside it is not difficult to see why and luckily, being so far above and away from the town, the church has not suffered the vandalism of recent restoration. Though built in the early twelfth century, St. Mary's was altered in the early seventeenth, the work being carried out by local shipwrights who gave the interior a 'between decks' battleship design that still remains. The interior is huge — it can seat 2000 people, though services have to be day–time only, there being no electricity — and contains a confused jumble of rare treasures. Do not, above all else, miss the box pews behind the triple–decked pulpit, one of which is a jade pew, a sort of church stocks for women, chiefly adulteresses, who walked to it bare–foot, to be sermonised on the need to repent and so serve as an example. Why did they put up with such humiliation?

On a happier note, seek out the Huntrodd memorial in a niche on an outside wall. Francis Huntrodd and his wife Mary shared the same birthday, 19 September 1600, and died within five hours of each other on that day, 80 years and 12 children later. The epitaph notes —

So fit a match surely could never be
Both in their lives and in their deaths agree.

The churchyard is a history of the brave seafarers of Whitby, the more so because some are salt–etched beyond reading. There is, perhaps, no better memorial to a dead sailor than a salt–rotted tombstone beside the sea.

Also in the churchyard is Caedmon's Cross, a memorial to the 'father of English sacred song', the country's first hymn–writer. Caedmon was a Northumbrian oxherd who slept with his charges. One night in the barn a stranger told him to sing the praises of the Lord and Caedmon found that he could, despite being unable to read or write. His story and his five songs — or poems, or hymns — came to the attention of St. Hilda, Abbess of Whitby, who brought him here as a poet and teacher. Caedmon became a monk and one day, as he lay in bed, he asked for the Eucharist. He was asked why, since he was not ill, but he took it, crossed himself and died. Caedmon's story is told by the Venerable Bede.

The Abbey Caedmon joined was not the building that stands in sight of his cross. In 655, in thanks for his defeat of the pagan King Penda of Mercia, Oswy of Northumbria founded 12 abbeys, one of which was here at Whitby. The Abbey was a joint house, monks and nuns, under the first Abbess St. Hilda, daughter of Hereric, a prince of Northumbria's Royal House; Oswy's daughter Elfleda was later Abbess. At that time the Abbey was known as Streonshalh, spelt that way or in one of any of half a dozen other ways. The name is probably derived from 'fari sinus', the bay of the watch-tower. Bede tells us this, and since it is likely that there was a Roman signal station on the cliff here, it would be quite an appropriate name.

In 664 King Oswy called a synod here, so that the Celtic and Roman arms of the Christian Church could decide upon the differences between them, in order to prevent disunity. The reason usually given for the synod is that it decided upon the appropriate method for fixing the date of Easter. This it did, but the problems between the two denominations were more profound than that. The Roman Church was rooted in martyrdom, the Celtic in evangelical conversion. That is a chasm too deep for this book to explore: suffice it to say the Roman Church emerged successful, shall we say — since victorious seems inappropriate.

Following the death of Bede, nothing of certainty is known of that first Abbey. Only a lead seal from around 660 exists as a truly tangible reminder of its existence: it was destroyed utterly by Danish raiders around AD 867, and the site lay waste for 200 years.

Around 1078 three men came this way: Aldwin, a monk of Winchcombe Abbey in Gloucestershire, and his companions Elfwy and Reinfrid. Reinfrid was deeply moved by the holiness of the spot, still, perhaps, with a few stones as reminder of St. Hilda. He asked for, and was given land by William de Percy, the Norman lord, and founded a Benedictine house. It was always a difficult spot; the house was horribly exposed, both to the ravages of the weather and those of North Sea raiders. Around 1153 'the king of Norway entered the port of Whitby with many ships, ransacked the goods of the monks, laid waste everything both within and without, and though he shed no blood yet he carried off with him whatever he could find, so that they who by the management of their abbot had grown very rich now became very poor, the rapacious Norwegians having left them nothing'.

Despite this, the Abbey rose again, becoming quite rich, a richness displayed in the Abbot's dinner service of 'silver, gilt with gold' noted in 1395. And though at the Dissolution, in December 1539, Whitby was one of the poorest of Benedictine houses, it was much richer than those of other, more simple, orders.

After the Dissolution, the roof was stripped of lead, the buildings then rapidly becoming derelict, a local quarry. The church bells were put on a ship bound for London, but the ship sank on a perfect day, still in sight of the Abbey and it is said that on some nights the sacred bells can still be heard from beneath the waves.

The further destruction of the Abbey ruins by the elements continued for centuries, each great storm causing the collapse of another major section. Then, on 16 December 1914, 375 years and 2 days after the Abbey's surrender, it was shelled by two German battleships and a cruiser. These ships had shelled the coast from Scarborough northwards, an attack that lasted three hours and cost 122 lives. At Whitby, the Germans aimed at coastal emplacements next to the Abbey, but struck the west front several times. In 1920, the Abbey passed to the Government and the ruins were made stable.

What remains on the clifftop now is all medieval: some remains of the Saxon Abbey were unearthed to the north of the present structure, but these have all been re–covered; there were some defensive works, some cells and a larger building. Clearly the early Abbey was typically Celtic, with monastic cells, a common refectory and one or more churches, all within a wall that both protected the nuns and monks and kept them separate from the common folk. Of the Saxon churches nothing visible remains; probably they lie below the medieval church.

What we see of that church is from the re–building after the Danish raid. Of the monastic building other than the church very little has been excavated but the work undertaken suggests that everything lay to the south of it. The church itself is a wonderful ruin, wind–battered, salt–etched, but still defiant. The east end, with its triple tier of lancet windows, is still a breath–taking sight.

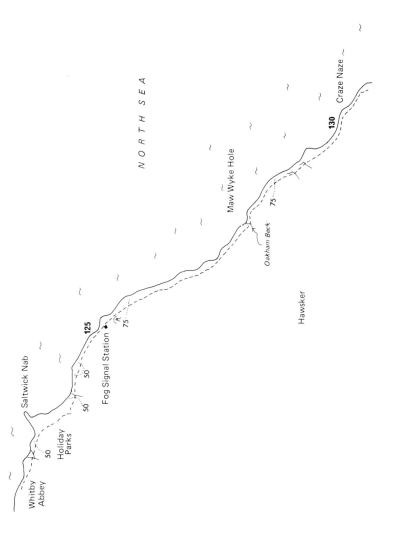

N O R T H   S E A

Craze Naze

130

Maw Wyke Hole

75

Oakham Beck

Hawsker

125

Fog Signal Station

75

Saltwick Nab

50

50

50

Holiday
Parks

Whitby
Abbey

50

It is also strangely gratifying to notice that the nave, to the west, and the presbytery, to the east, do not align correctly. In so many Abbey ruins, precision, elegance and magnificence seem almost supernatural. Here we can know that real men were involved, because they got their plan just a little bit wrong!

The Abbey was never a source of wonderful prosperity to the townsfolk in the way that some Cistercian houses were, but it was obviously awe–inspiring. It was said by some that if seabirds flew over its grounds, feathers fell from them; others said the birds themselves would fall from the sky, and noted that geese never over–flew the area. In 1611 one John Speed wrote '. . . There are certain fields here adjoining, where Geese flying over fall down suddenly to the ground, to the great admiration of all men.' Speed was, however, appalled by the 'superstitious credulity' of the people who misinterpreted this phenomenon as supernatural, claiming it was obviously a 'secret propriety of this ground, and a hidden dissent betwixt this soil and these Geese'! Since such stories are invariably based on a truth, or at least, on some truth, I wonder what happened here to conjure up a bird–abbey legend?

A more recognisable legend concerns St. Hilda and a plague of vipers that annoyed the builders and inhabitants of the early Abbey. With a great show of Christian love, St. Hilda cursed the snakes and they all crawled over the cliff to be petrified on the beach below. They are still there. John Speed again: '. . . Whitby, where are found certain stones fashioned like Serpents, folded and wrapped round in a wreath, even the very pastimes of Nature, who when she is wearied (as it were) with serious works, sometimes forgeth and shapeth things by way of sport and recreation'. Speed ridiculed the St. Hilda legend and so finished up being half right. The snake stones are ammonites, fossils from the Jurassic period.

The whole of the coast from here to the Way's end is a playground for the geologist and fossil–seeker, with a dozen or so types of shales, muds and limestones and a variety of fossils. But the tides are dangerous and wholesale vandalising of the cliffs

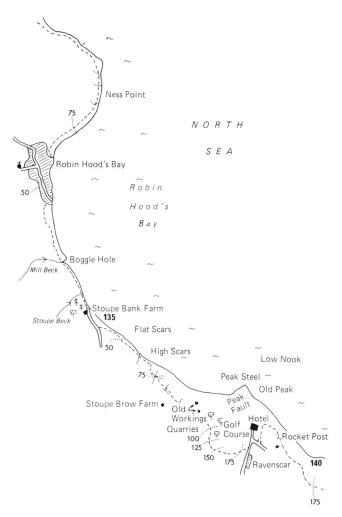

Ness Point

75

N O R T H

S E A

Robin Hood's Bay

50

R o b i n

H o o d ' s

B a y

Boggle Hole

Mill Beck

Stoupe Bank Farm

Stoupe Beck   **135**

Flat Scars

50

High Scars   Low Nook

Peak Steel

75   Old Peak

Stoupe Brow Farm   Old   Peak
                        Workings   Fault
                        Quarries   Hotel
                                100 Golf
                                     Course
                                125   Rocket Post
                                  150
                                       175   **140**
                                           Ravenscar

                                                        175

deplorable. At this stage, the Way is on the clifftop, and a more general note on the fossils will be held over until the beach is reached.

The Cleveland Way rejoins the clifftop path beyond Abbey Plain and continues to follow the edge to Saltwick Bay. Here coal–black Saltwick Nab lunges out into the sea, a rock spear that has impaled unsuspecting ships, none more famous than the *Rohilla*, a hospital ship en route for France in October 1914. She ran aground here in high seas and an epic rescue ensued over the next 50 hours, involving the hauling of lifeboats, and bravery and endurance by the crews almost beyond the limits of credibility. Of a total of 229 people on board, 145 were saved. Three Gold Medals of the RNLI were awarded, as were four silver medals.

The Way passes several caravan sites and, at (927 104), the outer perimeter wall of T'awd Bull, Whitby's foghorn. If it is foggy it might be worth waiting: the horn is deafening.

Beyond the foghorn, the path is straightforward all the way to Robin Hood's Bay, with views that become progressively more impressive as the Bay opens out. The cliff here is remote, the majority of holiday–makers staying closer to the town end–points, and the walker is almost assured of peace and quiet. He shares his day only with the birds, the stiff–winged fulmar, surely the finest flier of them all, the noisy kittiwakes, the delicate common gull and far–from–delicate herring gull. At the beach edge there will be the pied flash of an oyster–catcher with its distinctive bleep and out to sea, if the Wayfarer is lucky, common terns, with swallow tails and rapier beaks, diving for fish. If, instead, the Wayfarer comes this way in winter, he may catch sight of a ringed plover or turnstone working the beach anxiously, and out to sea an eider duck or the magnificent, seemingly painted not feathered, red–throated diver.

Even after the Wayfarer has turned the corner into Robin Hood's Bay, say at (959 061) above Ness Point, the town of the same name is hidden from view, tucked into a fold of cliff. When it is reached turn left to reach the old village, a collection of houses piled seemingly one on top of the other, all in a mad rush to climb the cliff and escape the sea.

Robin Hood's Bay

It seems unlikely that anyone visiting the town for the first time would not ask why it is named after a medieval outlaw from Nottingham. It is unfortunate, therefore, that the answer is that nobody knows. But there are legends.

One has Robin leaving Marion to live with a sailor's widow in Scarborough(!). French pirates then threaten the town and Robin creates such havoc on them with his longbow that they surrender, the townsfolk taking 6 tons of silver from their ship. It is said that Robin used part of this loot to endow a home for old sailors, but there is no historical evidence to support this.

Another story has Robin retiring here when he becomes too old or tired to continue his forest life, and keeping a boat in the bay in case a quick getaway were needed. The Abbot of Whitby is said to have asked Robin for help when Danes attacked the Abbey, and since it is known that a marauding Scots raiding party, around 1544, was attacked by three boatloads of very accurate archers, it may be that these two stories have combined. Near Whitby there is a Robin Hood's Stone, said to mark the spot where his arrow landed when shot during a victory feast, and there are Robin and Little John fields near it.

Closer to the Bay town there are Robin Hood's Butts, two Bronze Age burial mounds said to have been used for archery practice. There seems to be no legend that Robin lies in one of the mounds, an arrow–shot away from the bay, in keeping with the schoolboy suggestion that in his blood–let, weakened state his bow arm had lost all strength, so that to comply with his request to be interred where his last arrow landed it was necessary to bury him on top of the wardrobe. On a more mundane level, some have suggested that the Bay's name derives from an ancient forest sprite, also called Robin Goodfellow, while others see a derivation from Raif and Raven, which also gives us Ravenscar, at the other end of the bay. As can be seen, there are a lot of ideas, but no answers.

It is a matter of opinion, of course, but I think the Bay town is a prettier and more exciting place than Staithes, with which it is often compared. It is thus more worthy of the title of 'Clovelly of the North', even if such comparisons are to be disapproved of, implying, as they do, that the Devon village is perfect, all others however good, being mere shadows. On top of the cliff is a modern — well, Victorian — town that grew up around the railway station to cream off a little of the tourist traffic. But it is down at the cliff base, behind the new, huge, but already faltering sea–wall, that the real town lies, a maze of traffic–free ginnels or alleys, some steep and cobbled.

It is said that when a man married, a house was built in his or his in–laws' garden so that his wife would not be lonely when he was away at sea. It certainly seems likely. Every cottage has a small stairs window, a coffin–window, because the stairs were too steep to negotiate with a coffin. Each house, too, has its secret passages so that a cask of rum could go from sea to cliff edge without seeing daylight — or so it is said! Be sure to visit the local museum, housed in the old mortuary.

When the railway closed, in 1965, the town could have died too, but it has prospered on tourism and some fishing. It would be a tragedy if it were any other way.

From the town the Way continues along the cliff edge, but the better route, if tides permit, is to follow the beach at least as far as Boggle Hole — where those using Youth Hostels for accommodation will want to go inland anyway — or to Stoupe Beck. If tides do not permit, the path continues from the top of Flagstaff Steps, to the left at the end of Albion Street. Albion Street itself leaves The Dock, the lowest part of the town, the only spot now where the sea wall is breached to give access to the sea.

The beach in the Bay is a fine walk. The Bay has been a haven and a hazard to shipping for as long as men have sailed the coast: in 1586 it was marked — as Robinhoodes Bay — on the Mariners' Mirror, a series of Dutch North Sea charts. The wreck of the

Robin Hood's Bay

Visitor in 1881 that needed the man–handling of the Whitby lifeboat has been mentioned earlier, but equally spectacular was the wrecking of the *Cap Palos* in 1918. This five–masted schooner was carrying 25,000 square feet of sail but still failed to clear the rocks. She lay here for a year, finally being freed by blasting, only to sink off Scarborough three months later.

In the Bay, more than 500 species of marine life have been identified: brown and red seaweed, winkles and other shellfish, sea urchins and anenomes and crabs galore. But be sure to turn back all lifted stones and not to injure anything.

At (954 040) is the Boggle Hole, where Mill Beck reaches the sea. The old mill is now a Youth Hostel, the descent to which, if you are on the clifftop path, needs care, especially if it is wet. The name derives from a boggle or goblin, who lived here, but do not despair: he was, apparently, a helpful sprite if well treated. Nan, the local witch who could turn into a cat in order to climb the cliffs, was an altogether more unpleasant creature.

From Boggle Hole do not take the road going south–west from beyond the Mill Beck footbridge, but instead a path that leaves it almost immediately, south–east. This follows the cliff again and involves another messy descent to Stoupe Beck (958 036).

For those still on the beach their eyes should be not only on the tide, but also on the rocks, because of all the coast, this is the most famous area for fossils.

The fossils found here are the remains of animals that lived about 170 million years ago in the calm tropical sea beneath which the Jurassic rocks of the beach were laid down. Easy to spot are the ammonites, the coiled snakes of St. Hilda — indeed some of the types discovered here have been given the scientific name Hildoceras. But there are others: the ram's–horned Devil's Toenails, the gryphaea; bivalves; belemnites, originally squid–like creatures, now sharp crayons of rock; crinoids, plant–like starfish creatures; and, for the very lucky, plesiosaurs and ichthyosaurs. At Hayburn Wyke and in Burniston Bay, further along our route, dinosaur tracks have been found, large three–

Robin Hood's Bay from Boggle Hole

toed footprints, though no bones have yet come to light.

But a word of caution. Smashing at the rocks to retrieve fossils is vandalism. It is also dangerous and usually results only in a disappointing pile of rock. Please leave all embedded fossils alone, there are enough to be found in cliff-erosion debris. And watch the tide.

From the footbridge over Stoupe Beck, a stepped path climbs steeply to a road at Stoupe Bank Farm (958 035). Follow this for a couple of hundred yards until a path left (east) just before the cottage allows the Wayfarer to return to the cliff edge. The view forward to the headland of Ravenscar is excellent. It is to that headland that we also are going, following the cliff edge to the third field boundary, where a well–signed inland (south) detour is followed. Continue in straightforward fashion to reach a farm lane from Stoupe Brow Farm, over to your right (south), that is followed south–east.

At (973 020) the track passes between disused alum quarries to the right (south) and the Low Peak alum works to the left (north). Shortly after, at (974 018), the track splits, the Ravenscar Geological Trail bearing left, the Cleveland Way bearing right (south–east, then south). At (975 015) a disused railway track is met, the path running parallel to it, to emerge near the National Trust Centre at Ravenscar itself.

Ravenscar can also be reached by continuing along the beach from Stoupe Beck, climbing up the cliff on a steep path that forms part of the Geological Trail, at (979 025). The advantage of this route is that it allows a close view of the Peak Fault, a Tertiary period (35–million–year–old) rock fault that is almost knife–edged and is one of the best exposed faults in Britain; the pathway from the beach to the Raven Hall Hotel follows it closely. The geology of this area of beach is dealt with more fully in Appendix I.

Ravenscar was the site of another in the chain of Roman signal stations. Here, in 1774, a sandstone block was found inscribed: 'Justinian, governor of the province, and Vindician, general of the forces of Upper Britain for a second time, with the younger

Robin Hood's Bay from Ravenscar

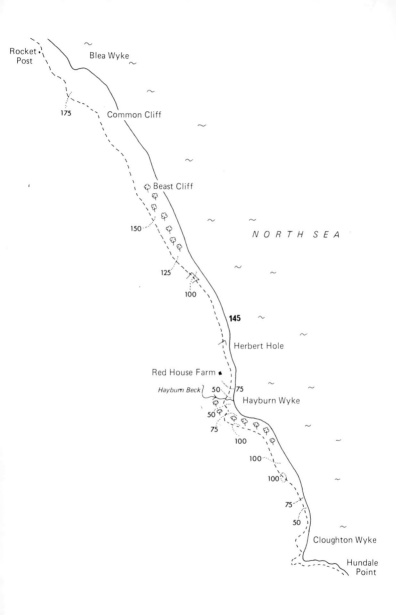

Rocket
Post

Blea Wyke

175

Common Cliff

Beast Cliff

150

125

100

145

Herbert Hole

Red House Farm

Hayburn Beck

50

75

Hayburn Wyke

50

75

100

100

100

75

50

NORTH SEA

Cloughton Wyke

Hundale
Point

provincial soldiers, built this fort, the manager of public works giving his assistance'. So, the idea of self–congratulatory foundation stone is nothing new!

But despite this Roman presence, it is believed that the name is Norse. The raven was Odin's secret bird, and the Danish sagas tell of the raising of a raven standard on a scar, a headland, of the coast. It has been suggested that this was a very early Danish beachhead, the dykes on the Moors inland having been dug by the newcomers to protect their boats and, therefore, their retreat.

Today the invaders carry golf clubs, and a very sporting course Ravenscar must be if a good stiff wind is blowing off the sea. The Raven Hall Hotel is the end point of the Lyke Wake Walk that joined us at Osmotherly and followed us to the high Moors. Those who are finishing successfully will have left Osmotherly less than 24 hours ago. With all our interim travels and exploration, it feels that the village should be further away.

The Cleveland Way passes the entrance to the Raven Hall Hotel, turning right (south–east) along Station Road, which it leaves to follow the hotel ground's wall towards the sea again. Ignore a track right, and continue to the cliff edge, going right (south–east) along it, staying close to the edge. A Coastguard rocket post is passed and on the beach below it, as we approach Blea Wyke, are some mermaids' tables, odd cylindrical, flat–topped lumps of resistant limestone from around which the softer shales have weathered.

At (991 008), near the Coastguard lookout, those blessed with good viewing weather should get their first view of Flamborough Head, which lies beyond Filey, the end–point of our route. Further along, near the aptly named Prospect House Farm (999 992), Scarborough Castle comes into view. The cliff here is Beast Cliff, a landslip formed into an initial steep section rising from the sea and a shallower section up to us, the two cliffs separated at half–height by a vegetated ledge. A path runs along this wide ledge, reached from the Coastguard lookout, and is a fine walk. At the base of the cliff, near the sea, is an often-sought grid reference, 000 000. Pity it is so difficult to reach!!

Just after Red House Farm (009 975), a stile is crossed and the Way descends through woodland to cross Hayburn Beck. The

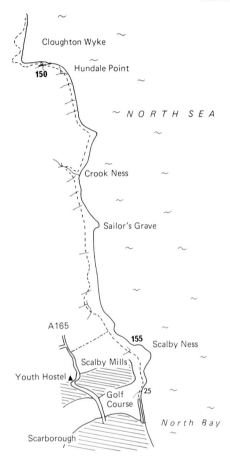

beck has carved a deep channel through the boulder clay, giving a very interesting geological exposure of the underlying rock. The steep and sheltered beck valley is wooded, and the beck reaches the sandy Wyke, a small cove, via a short bound over the exposed rocky lip. It is an interesting concentration of wildlife habitats, and is indeed a Nature Reserve, in the care of the Yorkshire Naturalists' Trust.

Beyond Hayburn Beck the cliff edge is regained and followed to another Wyke, Cloughton Wyke, a pretty shingle inlet protected by 100–foot cliffs. The view across to Hundale Point, a fine sea–bird nesting cliff, is magnificent. The Point itself is soon passed and, as we approach the Coastguard lookout (029 941), we leave the North York Moors National Park for the final time.

At Crook Ness (027 935) the Way heads inland using steps to cross a sea–reaching beck, and at Langhorn Wyke (029 928) there is a fine view into the cove, the northern point of which is called Sailor's Grave. The sailor is unknown — how sad to die a stranger here among such beautiful coastal scenery.

At (031 914) a signed path right (south–west) gives direct access to Scarborough Youth Hostel (left at the main road) and a camp–site (right at the main road). Straight on, the Cleveland Way descends to cross Scalby Beck and enter Scarborough.

Scarborough

Scarborough is a large seaside resort. For many who travel the long–distance footpaths of Britain, this is reason enough not to come here. In summer the backpacker can indeed feel far from comfortable among the jostling holidaymakers, but in winter the town is a quiet and interesting place.

Since it is so big, a detailed exploration of its sights is best accomplished along the town trails, details of which can be found in the Information Centre near the Grand Hotel. What is described here, after a look at the history of the town, is a straightforward walk along the seafront.

The town's history is ancient; there was an Iron Age village on Castle Hill. The Romans had a signal station here — the British Army Signal Corps is still here — but the name dates from later occupation. How much later is a matter of opinion. Does it derive from the Saxon, rock–fort; or from the Danish, skarthi–burgh, harelip's fort, a reference to hare–lipped Thorgils who came here with his brother Kormak in AD 966, a fact attested by the Norse *Kormakssaga*. It seems odd to me that anyone should be proud enough of a deformity to name his fort for it when he had a perfectly good name of his own; and there is, in any case, a history of Danish raids here, so why raid what you already own? We read that Harald Hardrada came to the Castle mound and fired the wooden town below it with flaming arrows. Even this sounds wrong: why, if he could take the mound, did he not have possession of the town already? Surely the townsfolk did not defend the town and not the mound? On balance I favour a Saxon name and a history of Danish raids, some successful enough to have resulted in the capture of the mound and the burning of the town.

There is no reference in Domesday to the town, so Hardrada's attack must have been very successful. However, the harbour here was too good and too well protected to be unoccupied for long, and we soon read of Scarborough again. In 1253, Henry III granted the town a charter to hold a fair which became known as

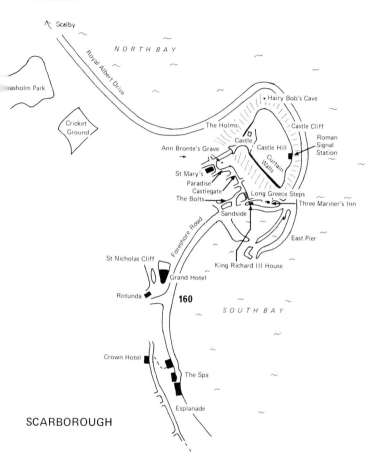

SCARBOROUGH

the gabler's or jabbler's fair, since, in part, it helped to pay the town's gablage, a tax on every house with a gable–end facing the street. The tax seems ludicrous to us now, but its imposition suggests a certain wealth in the town even at that early stage in its history. The fair was not only a market but included jugglers and minstrels, and is commemorated in a canticle of Simon and Garfunkel.

In 1346 the town sent one ship and 19 men to the siege of Calais, though in 1382 its involvement in the Wat Tyler revolt led to the imposition of a 900–mark fine. A hundred and fifty years later the same problems of helping the king on the one hand and rebelling on the other were seen again. In 1523 Henry VIII required all his subjects, aged 16 to 60, 'to be readye armed at an hour's warnynge to defend the sea costes from invasion by the Frenchman, and to keep good watche, and to have their beacons and other lyke tokens in readyness, in places accustomed'. But when Scarborough was besieged, in 1536, it was from inland, by an army led by priests during the Pilgrimage of Grace.

From that point on the town's history was dominated by the history of the Castle, until the end of the Civil War brought a peace that allowed real commercial growth. In 1730 Daniel Defoe came. He liked the town that was 'formerly famous for its strong castle, situated on a rock, as if it were hanging over the sea, but now demolished . . . Here there is such plenty of fish, that I have hardly ever seen the like . . . turbots here of three–quarters of a hundredweight, and yet they will cut exceeding well when new.' The harbour was obviously still bringing prosperity to the town.

By the early nineteenth century the town had its Spa, and things were improving quickly. The transition to seaside resort was made easily, and it is in that sense that most visitors know the town.

Our walk through Scarborough begins with the crossing of the beck that provided the power for the town's mill at Scalby. The mill, often damaged by flooding, was finally burnt down in 1821 in the absence of water to douse the flames!

Beyond is Royal Albert Drive — no prizes for guessing where the name came from. To the right are Peasholm Park, a very pleasant formal park, and then, in North Marine Road, the cricket club where Yorkshire plays an eight–day festival of cricket each year. Beyond these is an amusement park that offers good–looking wooden play forts and Europe's longest water slide, which is certainly worth a couple of minutes of anyone's time. To the left nothing remains of the North Bay pier, a piece of Victoriana that collapsed in 1901.

Royal Albert Drive swings left to the Castle mound and it is worth going up and right to the Castle entrance, as that allows the old church of St. Mary to be visited. Those who continue around the mound to the harbour see Hairy Bob's Cave, a face–like collection of holes on the seaward side of the mound. There are ancient tales of hermits at Scarborough, but as nobody knows who Bob was or even if the cave is old, speculation about it seems idle.

The Castle is approached by a walk from its west side. The mound it stands on is an impressive spot, a sandstone bastion amid the boulder clay, a last finger of moorland poking out into the sea. There was water on the mound too, a well 159-feet deep providing the first supply and a later one — deemed miraculous and called Our Lady's — finding water only 10 feet down. The mound is large, an 1823 survey giving its area as '43 a 1 r 16 p and parts' excluding 'the waste' covered by the buildings. It is unlikely to be that big today, as there is continuous erosion of the underlying sandstone.

The mound is 300 feet above the sea and 100 feet above the surrounding land, giving it a commanding view to which its steep sides added a natural defence. The Roman signal station was built to the same pattern as that at Goldsborough and was presumably abandoned at the same time, though there has been no evidence so far unearthed for a slaughter of the guards. It has nearly all disappeared now.

As we have seen, Harald Hadrada come this way in 1066 en route, with fellow chief Tostig, for defeat by Harold at Stamford Bridge. Harold's victory there may have been, in part, responsible for his subsequent defeat at Hastings, and the conquest of England by the Normans, his army being footsore and weary. Whether it was or not, the next inhabitants of the mound were Normans. The first Castle was built by William de

Gros, Earl of Yorkshire. To defend the mound a curtain wall was built on the landward side at the mound edge, and a keep was placed behind this, near to the narrow finger of connecting land that reached towards the wall gate. Later a barbican was built on the connecting finger, with a drawbridge over a constructed ditch. The building work produced a formidable fortification, as subsequent events were to show.

The Castle acted as a prison for Welsh and Scottish soldiers during the campaigns of Edward I, but it was not until 1312 that it was first besieged. Then it was held by Piers Gaveston, a favourite of Edward II but hated by the barons beyond the gate. The Castle proved impregnable but food ran out, and Gaveston had to surrender. He was offered safe conduct, but chivalry came a poor second to dislike, and he was taken prisoner and beheaded.

The Castle now decayed and was repaired in turn until 1537, when it was again under siege. Sir Robert Aske led the attack, commanding an army during the Pilgrimage of Grace. For 20 days Sir Ralph Eure held the Castle for his king on nothing but bread and water. Finally Aske was defeated, executed and hung in chains at York.

Next came Sir Thomas Stafford, attempting to wrest Queen Mary's crown on the basis of descent from Edward III. He landed here disguised as a peasant and with about 30 men seized the Castle. It was this action that gave rise to the expression a Scarborough warning. This is a word and a blow, but the blow first! Subsequent blows were less impressive, Stafford surrendering after one week and being executed for treason.

At about this time we have a description of the castle given by the traveller Leland: 'On the este end of ye toune, on the one poynt of the bosom of the see, where the haraboroure for shippes is, standith an exceedding goodlye, large and stronge castelle on a stepe rock, havinge but one way, by the stepe, slaty crag to cum to it.'

When Civil War broke out, Scarborough was held for Parliament by Sir Hugh Cholmley, but he changed sides early, when the Parliament leaders failed to come to terms with the king after the battle of Edgehill. However, not until January 1645, in the wake of Marston Moor, did the town come under direct threat. Then Sir John Meldrum arrived with 3000 Scots and besieged the town. Oliver's Mount, to the south of the town, is said to be named for the Cromwellian batteries brought to bear on the town from it, but it seems too far away to have played any real part in the battle. Gradually Sir Hugh was pushed out of the town and into the Castle. Sir John advanced to view the defences and the wind from the sea blew his hat off. He reached for it, was unbalanced by another gust and fell 'head foremost, down the cliff amongst the rocks and stones at least steeple height'. He lay speechless for three days but had recovered well enough six weeks later to be leading his men again. On 11 May 1645 he was wounded in the stomach and died on 3 June. But still Sir Hugh held out. The Castle was bombarded to such an extent that when, finally, the Royalists surrendered, a way had to be made through the rubble for them to march out. Sir Hugh had 20 of 200 men left unwounded: towards the end they had eaten cats, dogs, rats and even sparrows; they had boiled and chewed their leather belts; their teeth and hair were falling out from scurvy and they could barely stand, let alone walk.

Colonel Baynton, the new Parliament leader, was impressed by Sir Hugh's fortitude, but the womenfolk of Scarborough were not; they had to be restrained from stoning him for having so treated their husbands.

Baynton died and was replaced by his son, Colonel Matthew Baynton, who astonishingly, changed sides when the second Civil War siege started in 1648, so that Parliament had to take town and Castle again. During this siege, a townswoman sewing in her house was left unharmed when a stray shot destroyed the table she sat at, and the room around her. This siege was less severe than the first and Baynton surrendered when his exhausted men realised the task was hopeless. Remarkably, Baynton was not executed.

Parliament ordered the Castle slighted but there was no need, there being precious little left to slight. There was enough, just, to act as a prison for the Quaker George Fox, kept here from April to September 1665. He was held in a room without a fire and open to the weather, so that his fingers swelled up with the cold; he existed on a threepenny loaf every three weeks.

The last action here came in December 1914 when the German battleships *Derfflinger* and *Von der Tann* shelled the town and Castle, flattening an empty brick barracks beside the Castle and damaging the walls. In the town 19 people were killed.

Today the Castle is much as it was when the Civil War ended, and is well worth seeing, if only for the magnificent entrance gateway and bridge connecting town and mound, though the damage effected by wind and rain can be seen on the sandstone, which is pitted like Gruyère cheese. Enough of the keep remains to be impressive, and the curtain wall offers a fine walk with a good view to the old town and harbour from its southern end.

Had you been alive on 23 September 1779 the mound, which separates Scarborough's North and South Bays, would have been a fine vantage point from which to watch the sea battle between four ships under the command of the American privateer Paul Jones, aboard *Le Bonhomme Richard*, and two English Navy ships, *Serapis* under Captain Richard Pearson, and *Countess of Scarborough* under Captain Piercy. The English ships were protecting merchant vessels which, under the cover of the three–hour battle, gained the harbour. The battle was fought at night but the ships were so close in that by the light of gunpowder flashes men could be seen on board. So close were they, in fact, that several cannonballs hit the cliffs of the mound. The *Countess of Scarborough* was crippled first, but *Serapis* fought on, getting so close to the American's ship that their guns touched his timbers. The aft end was blown completely away and it was said there was not one foot of timber aboard that was not splintered. Not a man on the *Serapis* escaped serious injury and yet by morning the American victory, the two English ships being destroyed, was seen to be hollow: Jones had lost 300 men to the English 49, and his flagship sank, preventing him from landing as planned and causing him to leave the area. Not surprisingly, Captain Pearson was knighted.

In 1781 the Castle was prepared for a possible attack from

Harbour and Castle, Scarborough

sea–borne Frenchmen. The list of Ordnance taken in makes fascinating reading. There were 'wad hooks, with staves and rammers', 'hazel hooped budge barrells' and even '15 cwt of junk'! French prisoners were actually held in the town. A letter of 1799 from the town elders to London talks of three men 'so long confined'. The town would like to know if there is any chance of getting them transferred to 'Lynn, Yarmouth, Chatham or London . . . or any one of the established depots'. It could hardly sound more desperate if they had added 'or anywhere'!

Finally, it is said that the noise of the battle of Waterloo could be heard in Scarborough.

Close to the Castle entrance is St. Mary's, Scarborough's Parish Church. During the first Civil War siege it was used to house some of the Parliamentarian army's cannon and was, in consequence, bombarded from the Castle and half destroyed. The cost of repairs was estimated at £600, but this rapidly rose to £2,500 as wind and rain added to the devastation. Not for many years was the building finally restored. Inside it is solid, if a little unexciting, with some stonework remaining from the thirteenth–century Norman building.

The church is famous as the burial place of Anne Brontë, who died in lodgings on St. Nicholas Cliff in 1849 when only 29 and having completed only two books. Anne had come to Scarborough, as did many others, hoping the sea air would bring a miracle cure for her tuberculosis. It did not. Her simple, dignified tombstone lies at the top of a curiously empty grave–field opposite the church. Those who have walked from the Castle will have passed a small car-park on the left, before the church, on the wall of which a poor plaque offers the advice that 'Behind this wall lies the grave of Anne Brontë'. I am sure many believe she deserves a better message on a better plate.

At the bottom of Church Lane go left and along Paradise. The name derives from the walled garden below the site, used by Cistercian monks who 'owned' the church. Paradise House, to the right, is said to be the birthplace of Sir George Cayley, the 'father of Aeronautics', though he always maintained he was born in St. Nicholas Street! At the end of Paradise (!) turn down Castlegate and the Long Greece Steps to Quay Street, then left and along to the Three Mariners Inn. The inn is claimed to be the town's oldest, and is said to have been a favourite with smugglers, a claim supported by a number of secret cupboards and passages. It is also said to be haunted by the ghost of a headless woman, which seems appropriate for a building now converted to a museum of the town's bygone days.

Behind the Three Mariners is Sandside, and the harbour. As the best harbour for 50 miles south of Teeside, and having the advantage of being not on the Moors but on the plain, giving easy access to central England, Scarborough enjoyed considerable advantages. Ports always seem to attract wonderful characters, and Scarborough is no exception. I like the man who feigned imbecility in order to be flung off a ship he had been press–ganged on to; or Capper Jack, as strong as any four men, who bent a poker around the neck of one man who wanted to fight him and told him he might do so, when he had removed it; or the men who demanded to be excused war service in the last century, on the grounds that anyone 'whose house lets in rain, whose chimney carries not out smoke and whose wife is never quiet should be exempt from going to the wars'! The harbour we see today dates from the early nineteenth century and is still used for bulk cargo and by a small fishing fleet.

Be sure to notice, as you pass Richard III's house, reputedly where he stayed during several visits to the town, the stone effigy of the king behind its protective grille.

Beyond Sandside, Foreshore Road, is Scarborough's 'Golden Mile' of amusement arcades etc. But first, behind the cafés, visit The Bolts, a fine series of narrow alleyways dating from the twelfth century when they were the public toilets, flushed twice daily by the North Sea. In such narrow passages as this — though not when they were lavatories — lived Scarborough's wise men, who could see all and cure much. It is a strange fact that until the last decade of the nineteenth century there were still such men in the town. A notice from around then, posted in Staithes, says: 'stolen yesterday afternoon, a large fisherman's net belonging to Jack. If it is not brought back before tomorrow at one o'clock he'll apply to the wise men at Scarborough'.

On the left we pass the small fish market, a delightful place, and then Scarborough's lifeboat, the most accessible of all those we have passed. Two of its crew died in 1861, the year of the Whitby tragedy. That was a terrible year, with an estimated 778 ships wrecked on the British east coast, from Pentland Firth to Dungeness. During its lifetime, from the first boat in 1800, the Scarborough boat has saved over 1000 lives, with a loss of 15 crewmen. The debt owed to these men is incalculable.

Scarborough was very quick to transfer its energies to the new pastime of sea–bathing when the delights of taking the waters began to pall. It even made a virtue of reality, advertising itself as being 'many degrees cooler in the month of August than at Brighton, and possibly than at Weymouth, or any place south of the Thames'. Scarborough was, simply, the best place in Britain for sea–bathing, being 'clean and neat . . . some distance from the opening of a river . . . highly loaded with sea salt and the other riches of the ocean . . . not weakened by mixing of fresh water with its waves . . . shore, sandy and flat, for the convenience of going into the sea in a bathing chariot . . . bounded by lively cliffs and downs'. As an early nineteenth–century writer noted, how could anyone 'voluntarily prefer to it their Margate, their Brighton and their Hastings. O for more taste and better judgement!'

Sea–bathing was recommended for nervous complaints, St. Vitus's dance, hysterical and hypochondriacal disorders, general debility and just about everything else. The bathing chariots had canvas extenders to protect the bather from prying eyes as he entered the water, and one of them had, printed on the side —

> When old bards sung, of Venus sprung
> From foam — great Ocean's Daughter;
> They meant to show what beauties owe
> To bathing in salt water

Of course when the railway came in 1845, so did *hoi polloi*. They brought cash and prosperity, but the seaside town's founding fathers never really got over it.

Beyond the new holiday façade St. Nicholas Cliff is reached, where Anne Brontë stayed, and where the Grand Hotel stands.

Pevsner said of it that it was 'wondrous . . . a High Victorian gesture of assertion and confidence, of denial of frivolity and insistence on substance than which none more telling can be found in the land'. Little more needs to be said, really, except to add that in its heyday the hotel was reckoned to be the finest in Europe.

Close by is the Rotunda Museum, built in 1829 by the Scarborough Philosophical Society to house a fossil collection, in part as a memorial to William Smith, town–born and the 'father of English Geology'. Smith had discovered a relationship between rock strata and fossil remains, and the museum illustrated this with shelves rising up the wall. Of course, the top shelves could not be seen from the ground (!), a matter resolved in 1838 when £6.10s was expended on a four–wheeled, hand–propelled moving platform. Even this did not entirely overcome the museum's problems though, because the only windows, high up, had been made deliberately tiny to reduce the sunlight that, it was feared, might harm the exhibits. The window design was based on Rome's Temple to the god Ridiculoso. The unkind maintained that the god was behind the whole edifice. Today the wheeled platform survives but does not operate, but the Rotunda is still a museum, now of local history.

Further into the town the visitor can find Charles Laughton's birthplace; see 'The Crescent' one of the highlights of Scarborough's architectural heritage; visit the Wood End Natural History Museum; or rub shoulders with Charles Dickens's ghost in the Assembly Rooms. It all seems so genteel, in keeping with the Spa ahead, and the calm summer sea to the left. Unless you are here on a storm–lashed day, that is. One Scarborough storm, in 1829, was so bad a town resident shot himself.

The Spa building is reached at the southern end of Foreshore Road. In 1626 a Mrs. Farrer, 'a Gentlewoman of good Repute', noted brown–stained stones under a stream flowing into South Bay. She tasted the water and found it acidic. She claimed a 'medicinal quality' and told her friends; the foundations of the 'Queen of Watering Places' had been laid. Colonel Fairfax, the Parliamentarian leader, tried the waters in 1660, but it was not until the century's end that the first cistern was built. That first

Spaw (the invariable local spelling) house was destroyed by a landslip in 1737; a proper pump room was then built. It was noted that 'the diversions are pretty much on the same footing as at Bath'. Like Bath the Spa had a governor or master of ceremonies, though Dicky Dickinson has never become a name to rival Beau Nash. He never did as well at the job, either, having to supplement his income by cleaning shoes.

Rules were, of course, laid down for taking the waters. It was best to do so from May to September when they were undiluted by winter's rain. After arriving, the taker rested for two or three days. Then he or she rose early to be at the Spaw by 6 a.m. to drink two or three half–pints. This quantity rose gradually until nine or ten pints were being drunk! And all before noon, 'lest if the meat mix with the water, it do float in the stomach and be washed down into the bowels unconcocted'.

The Spa waters were claimed to be excellent for 'drying up superfluous humours' and were extolled in print several times, firstly by a Dr. Wittie in 1660, but most elegantly in a book of 1670 by Dr. George Tunstall called *Scarborough Spa Spagyrically Anatomised*. Later still, Dr. Peter Shaw, soon to become physician to George III, noted that the waters were 'formerly known to few and healing chiefly the sick of inferior rank . . . introduced into better company and now clear the spirits and brace the nerves of Peers as well as commoners'. That must have been a great comfort to the workmen who dug the stream out of the landslip on a no–waters–no–pay basis.

Scarborough rose in popularity — Sheridan wrote a play about it — but never quite made it to the very pinnacle. Harrogate proved to be very strong local competition and even when the waters' mineral salts were collected by evaporation and bottled, Epsom salts were there just before to corner the market. The magnificent Spa buildings we have reached date from the mid–nineteenth century, though there have been considerable developments in this century, most recently between 1979 and 1985. Behind the most northerly building of the complex is a path

Scarborough Spa

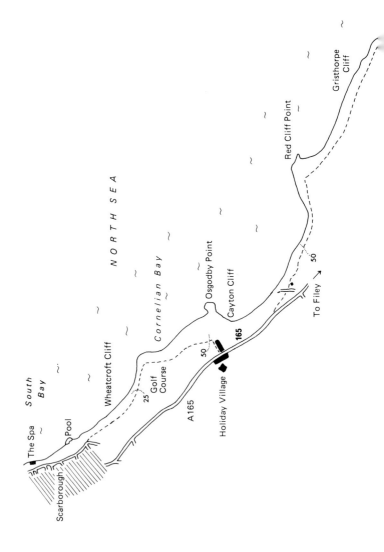

Gristhorpe Cliff

Red Cliff Point

N O R T H   S E A

Cornelian Bay

Osgodby Point

Cayton Cliff

50

To Filey

South Bay

Wheatcroft Cliff

Golf Course

A165

Holiday Village

165

50

25

The Spa

Pool

Scarborough

up the cliffs. Take this to The Esplanade, a fine row of buildings built around the same time as the new Spa buildings. The hotels here have a fine view out over South Bay and the old town.

We leave Scarborough southward along The Esplanade. Below is an open–air swimming pool beyond which a path leaves the road for the cliff edge. Behind us now, Scarborough fills the landward arc of South Bay. Let us leave it with a final quote — 'Our winters are milder than places in the same parallel of latitude (52°17′N) whose situation is more inland. It is universally observed that frost is less severe near the sea . . . Snow is often seen to cover the neighbouring hills, when we have scarce one atom within a mile of the shore. Strangers who have spent the winter at Scarborough have been surprised to find so mild a temperature prevails . . . Many families take up their residence here at that season of the year, when there is much social enjoyment and exchange of the courtesies and civility of private life'. You see, even in the late eighteenth century, Scarborough was better in winter.

The Way travels on the seaward side of the golf course to the cliffs above Cornelian Bay, named for the mineral which the very lucky visitor might find. Then the cliff walk is interrupted by a Holiday Village, which forces the Wayfarer right (south–west) to the main road at (059 853). Go left (south–east) along the road until at (063 846) a path to the left allows the cliff edge to be regained by crossing a couple of fields and a private road. From here to Filey Brigg the Way is easy to follow, and should be a joy, with good scenery and the satisfying knowledge that the Cleveland Way is nearly complete. Not that we want it to end; it is just that completion is a further reward. Sadly, the barbed wire near the holiday sites and the wind–blown rubbish give these last few miles a desolate air. Why are people so unconcerned with their own environment that they can treat it this way? And why, having paid money to go to one of the sites, do they need wire fences to keep them in?

At Newbiggin Cliff (100 827) the old boundary between the North and East Ridings of Yorkshire reached the sea. Beyond is

North Cliff, and then the sharp point of Filey Brigg.

Some say that the Devil decided to build a bridge from Yorkshire to Europe and started to pile rocks into the sea near Filey. He had only gone about a half–mile from the cliff line when he dropped his hammer. Feeling for it in the sea, he grasped a haddock, the fish still shows his thumb–print. But he did not find his hammer and gave up in disgust. The Brigg is the Devil's Bridge. Others know the truth. They recall Billy Biter, a local henpecked tailor, whose wife made the sweetest, stickiest parkin for miles. Billy was idling on the clifftop when he fell down a gully and disturbed a dragon lying on the beach. Billy gave the dragon his parkin. The dragon was so impressed he decided not to eat Billy but to send him home for a second piece. Billy's wife was so proud, she baked her best-ever parkin, and together the Biters returned to the beach. The dragon put the new cake into his mouth all at once and began to chew. But the sticky parkin glued his jaws together and later, exhausted and desperate, he pitched forward into the sea and drowned. In time his body became a skeleton, and the skeleton is Filey Brigg.

There is a nature trail on the Brigg — a leaflet for which, incidentally, speaks of boulder clay erosion and hard rock rib remains, but does not single out the dragon for mention — and it is easy to see why, when you descend the cliff path to the Brigg rocks. There are fossils on the Brigg, though not perhaps as many as at Ravenscar. There are shells lived in and vacant, seaweeds, and the clay cliffs are used by sand–martins, which certainly add interest to a summer visit. Further out, where the sea–cover is more frequent, the rock has been etched into a curiously woven texture, and it is here that sea anenomes and urchins are to be found. There are marvellous rock pools, one so large it has even been named the Emperor's Pool, reputedly for the Roman Emperor Constantine. Is this a folk memory from the time when the Romans had a signal station on the cliff at the back of the Brigg?

But please be careful at the sea's edge. There are many stories of people being taken by surprise here, by swift tides or large waves from placid seas. Not all the stories have a happy ending.

Our route into Filey, our terminal town, will be along the beach

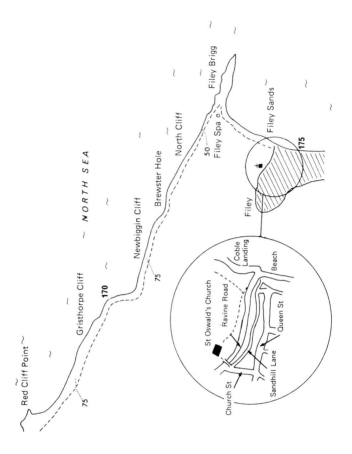

if the tide is out, along the cliff if not. It is as well to leave before
dusk: the Brigg is haunted by the ghosts of sailors whose ships
were impaled on its rock spear. The Bay here, enclosed by the
Brigg and distant Flamborough Head, is a beautiful seaside spot,
6 miles of pebble–less flat sand. But, as with all of the coast we
have travelled, it is a brutal, unforgiving spot when a high sea is
running. There is a long history of tragedy here.

Those on the beach reach first the coble landing in old Filey.
The cobles here are as we have seen before, slightly modified and
lightened for beach–launching. An 1876 plan to blast the Brigg
into a harbour was greeted with jubilation by the townsfolk, but
nothing came of it.

As with any occupation where there is a high degree of
objective danger, superstitions grew up around the local fishing.
Black cats were unlucky here, and no man would fish if he saw
one, or a pig, on the way to his boat. At sea whistling was not
allowed: you could whistle up a storm. There was also a curious
local custom of slitting a net cork and fixing a coin in the slit. It
was said that the custom was Danish and related to the paying of
a fishing tax to the King of Denmark, but it seems more likely to
be a tribute to the sea gods, like the ritual at nearby Flamborough
where a coin was tied to an arrow shot out to sea.

But hard though it may have been, and beach–hauling the
cobles at Filey has never been easy, the life bred wonderfully
tough, if sometimes rough, men. Preachers from Bridlington who
came to Filey in the early 1880s received hard–thrown old fish in
exchange for their new ideas, but a Wesleyan chapel was built
and cobles with names like *Good Intent* became more common.

Beyond the cobles is our final lifeboat, a far cry from the first
boat, a 30–foot, 12–oared rowing–boat bought in 1823 for £98. It is
worth noting that that date, 1823, precedes Grace Darling's
famed rescue by 17 years. It was her daring that fluttered the
Victorian heart and caused the 'Shipwreck Institution' to be
formed, leading to the formation of the RNLI in 1860, but the
seafaring men of Filey needed no such example, fine though it

Coble landing and Brigg, Filey

was, to give them their lead. Beside the lifeboat is an In–shore Lifeboat, a rubber inflatable designed to be quick enough to go to the aid of weekend sailors in the bay.

In front of the Wayfarer, as he passes the lifeboat and arrives at the end of the coble landing, is Filey seafront. But do go right, either up Ravine Road or up the paths on its right–hand side, to visit the church.

At the church the clifftop route joins the beach route. The cliff Wayfarer has passed, without noticing, the nothing that now remains of Filey Spa. It was a spring of water, 'colour — whitish; contains, besides iron, a considerable proportion of sea salt, some Epsom salt, calcareous earth, and probably much fixed air'. The water was claimed to have effected 'many astonishing cures', being especially good with 'windiness' and 'hypochondrial melancholy'. I wonder how many people were willing to admit they suffered from the latter?

Filey Spa never succeeded. If glorious Scarborough failed to compete with Harrogate, what chance did this little place stand?

The church is named for St. Oswald, a Northumbrian saint who took the gospel to Lincolnshire and may, therefore, have passed close to Filey. Pevsner called it the finest in the north–east corner of the West Riding, and was impressed by its exterior, the 'impressively direct outline' and 'powerful tower'. It is true, the church does have great presence. That at Whitby may be impressive because it is set four–square against the elements, but St. Oswald's shows us the charm of a tree–filled backdrop. Not that it is anything but a coastal church: salt is in the air, and has etched the tombstones just as surely — look at the fine memorial in the churchyard corner, built like a summerhouse. You need to work hard to trace the family name in the salt–crumbled rock.

The church represents an almost complete Norman structure, the earliest work from around 1180, the latest from around 1250. The interior is interesting because it appears that the builders changed their minds several times. There is no central aisle, which is not all that common, and the columns at either side are

St. Oswald's Church, Filey

round here, octagonal there, unique in my experience. On the south wall is a rough statue, about two feet high, which may be a memorial to a boy bishop. Boy bishops were elected by the parish boys to act as bishop within the church from St. Nicholas Day (6 December) to Christmas Eve. It is thought that if an elected boy died in office a miniature effigy would be produced for him, though originally it would probably have been mounted horizontally. Other experts, notably Pevsner, contend that the effigy marks a heart burial. Such burials were common when manorial lords owned land in several parts of the country: after death their hearts were removed and other parts of them, so that something could be buried in each of the estates. Since no evidence for the effigy is available other than the date, around 1250, from the carving style, it is not possible to make a final decision.

Leave the church on a path heading north of west to cross a fine old iron bridge giving a lovely view down the wooded ravine. It is difficult to believe that 100 years ago the ravine was bare of trees, having been landscaped by the town council. The 'ancient' view is therefore much less ancient than in Church Street beyond the bridge.

In the Domesday Book, Filey is 'Fucelac' which could be from 'wildfowl meadow' or from 'finger of land', either of which description fits the area tucked in close to the Brigg. Brigg itself is Danish, and means a landing place, though it is also the root of the more obvious 'bridge'. What we see here in Church Street and in Queen Street reached by a left turn, is much more recent than the name. The local museum is housed in what is believed to be the oldest building apart from the church, dating from the late seventeenth century. While you are in Queen Street look also for the terraced cottages with coloured door panels depicting fishing scenes. Here too you will find T'awd Ship, the old inn, with a good collection of smuggling stories. At the street–end, the lamp has a red panel facing seaward to help the local fishermen fix their position at night.

As Queen Street ends we can go right to reach 'new' Filey, a Victorian seaside resort the best of which is to be seen in The Crescent, which is distinctly non–crescent shaped. In Rutland

Street lived Dr. E. Pritchard, the surgeon who wrote a local guide in 1856 but is better remembered for being the last man to be publicly executed in Scotland. After leaving Filey for Glasgow he murdered his wife and mother–in–law, and was hanged before 100,000 people in 1865. On a happier note, in Belle Vue Street is Brontë Cafe, once Cliff House, and visited by Charlotte Brontë. She liked Filey but feared that the growth of guest houses would ruin its quiet serenity. The growth had arrived in the wake of the railway and of John Wilkes Unett, a Birmingham solicitor who recognised the area's potential, bought land and developed the resort. Unett was not the first developer here. In a Scarborough guide of 1787 one J. Schofield noted that though Filey was a difficult and precarious horse–ride away, it 'affords a novel and striking exhibition of the hoarse, rough sea, as it lashes the sandy shore at the foot of those cliffs as you pass very near the brink of'. Now that may not seem excellent grammar, and I wonder whether Schofield was referring to the bay's white 'hoarses', but it is no bad description of a stormy Filey Bay.

The quote leads naturally to another, a description of sea–bathing given in 1828 when Filey, having failed as a spa, was promoting itself as a resort: 'When a healthy person plunges into the sea, he feels a considerable shock or chill, and on rising from the waves a sobbing succeeds, the skin is contracted and feels rough to the hand, a cracking noise is heard, followed by a ringing or whizzing in the ears; on quitting the water, if it be done quickly, the nose discharges a pellucid rheum, tears sometimes fill the eyes, and saliva the mouth, and many persons experience a little shudder — but before the dress can but put on, a warm glow succeeds, the spirits are raised, all the sensations are agreeable, every motion light'.

All of that may be true, but I am slightly surprised that anyone ever reached the pleasant phrases, preferring to tear up the brochure after the opening lines.

Filey marks the end of the Cleveland Way, though it is the start of the Wolds Way that goes on south to the Humber. We have completed a fine walk over moor and along coast. Let us feel a

trifle smug and end with a note about Victorian Filey. It would be
of no interest, the note maintained, to 'the Cockney traveller who
drives about to stare at things in the north; to the fashionable
loungers at such a place as Scarborough; to the inhabitants of
inland towns, who rattle away in what they call a pleasant jaunt;
in short, to those who have no taste for simple pleasure, and who
find no enjoyment but in large companies, constant noise, and
endless changes of person and scenery, this place can have no
charms; but to those who possess a relish for the pure exhibitions
of nature, and take with them a little society, this place seems
well adapted as a summer resort, for soothing the mind, and
invigorating the body'.

   The language is a little intemperate, but many walkers may feel
a certain sympathy with the ideas expressed. It was written about
Filey but, with reservations about things that could have been
better put, it also fits the Cleveland Way.

Appendix I   The geology of the Way

For the most part, the Cleveland Way follows the borders of the North York Moors National Park, an upland region with well–defined physical boundaries. It rises from the Vale of Pickering to the south, the Vale of York to the west, and to the north the valley of the Tees and the North Sea, the latter also forming its eastern border. Within this region are clearly discernible areas, their differences, in the shape of the land and its usage being, to a large extent, dependent on the nature of the underlying rocks and the natural processes they have experienced.

The through–valley of the rivers Leven and Esk forms a natural division of the area, separating the northern moors from the principal moorland to the south and centre of the Park. This principal moorland consists of many smaller moors, typically named after adjacent dales. These frequent, winding dales cut deep into the upland to expose soils suitable for agriculture, and their fertile shelter provides a sharp contrast with the higher, bleak moors. To the north the dale–borne streams drain into the Esk Valley, for instance along Westerdale and Glaisdale, while to the south longer dales such as Bransdale, Farndale, Rosedale and Newton Dale drain to the Vale of Pickering through the Tabular Hills. These hills are named from the way the dales have cut steep–sided valleys that effectively separate the hills into tabular blocks. The Tabular Hills provide the southern boundary of the Park, with a steeply rising, north–facing limestone escarpment, and a gentle fall into the Vale of Pickering. The westernmost dale, Ryedale, separates the Tabular Hills from the Hambleton Hills with their west–facing escarpment. To the east, in common with the central moors, there is a gradual fall in height, the moorland becoming increasingly more dissected before reaching the coast in cliffs broken occasionally by sandy bays. This coastal region appears more agricultural than might be expected from the moors inland, due to a covering of fertile glacial deposits. The Cleveland Hills border the north–west of the Park in an escarpment that overlooks the Tees Valley and the Vale of York. Their highest point, on Urra Moor, at 1490 feet, is also the highest in the Park.

The rocks of the North York Moors had their origins during what is known as the Jurassic period of geological time, which began about 190 million years ago. It succeeded the Triassic period which started about 225 million years ago and was followed by the Cretaceous period 136 million years ago, during which the rocks forming the chalk hills of southern England and the Yorkshire wolds originated. These periods constitute the Mesozoic Era, a geological transition time during which the relatively primitive animals and plants of the Paleozoic era developed towards the more modern forms of the Cainozoic era.

The Jurassic rocks of the Park are sedimentary in nature, having been formed from sediments deposited on sea–beds or in river deltas that once covered the area. Such sediments are found as layers, strata — each layer having been deposited under different conditions which have, in consequence, produced a different type of rock. In the North York Moors there is a relatively straightforward geological structure, there being at most only gently sloping strata with few faults, and valleys that are clearly formed by erosion, complicated only by the effects of glaciation.

Earliest in the succession of sedimentary strata found here are the Liassic rocks, which lie beneath the whole area and which were long ago deposited as sand or mud at the bottom of the sea. The conditions in which these rocks were laid down were most favourable to fossil formation, and the area is well known for the abundance of fossils in the Jurassic strata. Fossils are the shell and skeletal remains of animal life or the carbonised remains of plants that have been covered and compressed in sediments, and so preserved. They yield much information about themselves and their living conditions, and also allow the identification of rock types. The fossilised remains of sea creatures, such as ammonites, are numerous enough in these rocks to allow the identification of at least three main Lias types. The occurrence of these around Whitby, and hence the abundance of the fossils, led to the inclusion of ammonites in the Abbey crest.

The Lower Lias and Upper Lias consist mainly of shale, a rock that is similar to slate but softer, while the Middle Lias has sandstones and ironstones within it. It was on the use of the latter that the now extinct Cleveland iron industry was founded, and evidence of ironworking is left in most places where the Middle Lias outcrops, for instance at the northern edge of the Cleveland Hills around Guisborough. The Upper Lias was also economically useful, yielding jet, alum and iron ore. Jet has been used for ornaments since the Bronze Age and occurs sporadically in a black shale known as the jet rock, that lies beneath the alum shale. The mining of both jet rock and the alum shale, along the north–west escarpment and the coast, is much in evidence along the route. Iron ores from the Dogger, the earliest of the mid–Jurassic rocks of the region, were the basis of the nineteenth–century Rosedale iron industry.

The Dogger developed from sediments deposited in shallow seas formed after the gentle folding of the Liassic rocks, which were then covered by the deposits of a huge delta that extended over the whole area during mid–Jurassic times. These deltas also produced the sandstones of the moorlands, and the remains of the vegetation that grew at that time are seen in the rocks, as well as in the coal seams that built up from them. The Park moorland lies on the poor soils produced from these rocks, which cover much of the Park area except where it is cut through by dales or is covered by younger rocks, and forms all or part of the coastal cliffs from Scarborough northwards. The rocks are known, not surprisingly, as the Deltaic series, and produce sandstone suitable for building, since it cuts easily into blocks. Marine sediments, identifiable from fossils, occur within this series, yielding evidence of three invasions of the delta by the sea, producing the Eller Beck Bed, the Mellepore Bed of the southern park, and the largest, the Scarborough Bed; these can be 100 feet thick and occur throughout the moorland area and along the coast.

A further invasion of the sea brought about the conditions in which the Upper Jurassic rocks were produced. Shallow sea deposits formed thick limestones and sandstones, the earliest beds of which are only seen in the northern moors and on the lower slopes of the northern scarp face of the Tabular Hills. They include the Kellaways rock, a ruddy sandstone, and the Oxford clay. Above them are the limestones of the Corallian series that are responsible for the landscape of the Tabular Hills and the south–western escarpment of the Hambleton Hills. This is an Oolitic limestone consisting of small rounded grains, known as ooliths, that have been cemented together, along with numerous fossils such as ammonites, suggesting a warm, clear, shallow sea.

It was in deeper seas that the Kimmeridge clay, now only remaining in the Vale of Pickering, was deposited. Apart from glacial and recent deposits, these are the youngest rocks found in the Park, although the region was once covered with Cretaceous chalk, the nearest remains of which are seen in the Yorkshire wolds.

Our geological knowledge of the area between the Cretaceous period and the latest Ice Age is somewhat uncertain. The Alpine earth movements that had their greatest effect around the Mediterranean had only slight, but definite, effects here, in folding the rocks into domes and dishes, the biggest of which is the Cleveland Dome of the central moorland. The whole area beneath the surface is made up of variously sized uplifts separated by their associated downfolds, though the form of the land as a whole is a result of the intense erosion that it subsequently underwent. The uniform level of the high ground in all of East Yorkshire suggests that it was under the smoothing action of the sea over a long period. Some more uplifting then followed, which established the basis of the radial drainage pattern with streams flowing away from the central moorland and cutting through to the underlying Lias to form the dales.

The processes of erosion have removed all traces of the chalk and much of the Kimmeridge clay that once covered the Park, and have further removed most of the softer Oxford clay to leave the limestone escarpment of the Tabular Hills. These processes continue to shape the land, the effects of marine erosion being particularly easily seen at several points along the coast.

The final major influence on the shaping of the land–forms seen today began about 2 million years ago, with a deterioration in the climate which brought about the glaciation of much of Britain during the Pleistocene period. These glacial conditions declined three times, leaving little to be seen today, but a fourth glaciation left numerous deposits, especially around the edges of the Park where much of the Way is traced.

As this last glaciation developed, ice flows from ice caps in the Lake District and the Scottish Highlands approached the North York Moors, which were too low to develop their own caps but large enough to deflect the two encroaching flows, and a third, the Scandinavian ice from the North Sea, though the latter did encroach inland along the coast. The Park was covered by snowfields and surrounded by ice everywhere except to the south, a situation that impeded drainage to the lowlands when the ice and snow began to melt. The meltwater was forced to form glacial lakes in the blocked moorland valleys before overflowing and eventually escaping by cutting meltwater channels or spillways. In this way a lake built up in the Upper Esk Valley and the valleys running into it, between the ice at Kildale to the west and Lealholm to the east, and beneath it were laid down the typical flat and fertile deposits of a glacial lake. Water from this lake escaped around the edge of the ice towards the Goathland area, where good examples of overflow channels are to be found. It is typical of such glaciated areas that the meltwaters cut channels unrelated to the preceding drainage pattern. The meltwater developed into another lake in the Fen Bog area, which then overflowed to cut Newton Dale. Similarly, a glacial lake developed in the Hackness Valley near Scarborough to overflow and cut Forge Valley. Together with the other waters that still traverse the Tabular Hills, these outflows drained the central moorlands of their meltwaters and deposited glacial sediments in the ice–dammed lake that covered the Vale of Pickering.

As the ice retreated, it left behind deposits made up from the debris it had carried. One localised land–form, originating from the front of a glacier, is known as a terminal moraine, as is seen at Lealholm. On a larger scale, the coastal belt is covered in a layer of red–brown clay hiding the pre–glacial features. This clay is commonly known as boulder clay, since it contains scattered rocks, often known as eratics, that can be used to indicate which direction the ice came from if they are known to be from a particular area. Rocks from the Lake District, Scotland and

Scandinavia have been found along the coast.

Away from these glacial deposits the Way begins at Helmsley on hills formed of the youngest remaining rocks found in the Park. The underlying Corallian limestones are responsible for the character of the Tabular Hills that stretch eastwards to the coast, and of the Hambleton Hills to the west. From these rocks has developed a fertile brown soil most suitable for arable farming, with much land given over to cereals, whilst beneath the fields is found the building stone so evident in the light grey, dry–stone walling and the cottages of villages such as Cold Kirby. Local quarries are still active, one of the few industries still using the Park's natural resources.

Having crossed the plateau we reach and follow the edge of the west–facing escarpment with its views over the Vale of York. The relatively resistant limestones of the hills form steep cliffs at the top of the scarp face, the succession of the other Jurassic rocks below not always being visible. From Sutton Bank the view is enhanced by the sight of Gormire, a lake formed in a glacial spillway after it had been blocked by a later mudflow.

To the north is Black Hambleton, the highest point of these hills, and there we pass on to heather moors more typical of the areas found on the sandstones of the Deltaic series that underlie the high moorlands. From Osmotherley onwards these sandstones top the scarp slope of the Cleveland Hills, with the Upper Lias outcropping below. On Urra Moor the Way climbs to the highest point in the Park, from where a broad ridge is apparent, falling gently away to the east. It is from this ridge that the general drainage pattern radiates, with dales cutting through the sandstones, often leaving cliff edges, to the Lias rocks below.

Waters running to the north flow into the Esk Valley that, in conjunction with the valley of the River Leven, dissects the Park. The Way crosses this incision at Kildale which, during the Ice Age, was as far as the ice extended into the valley from the west, and was thus the eastern extent of the lake that formed when the ice began to melt. Around the escarpment the meltwaters cut many overflow channels, several of which the Way uses or crosses. Scarth Nick, where the Drove Road climbs on to Osmotherley Moor, is one such channel, and others occur at

Carlton Bank where the waters ran into Bilsdale; Gribdale Gate, to the north between Kildale and Roseberry Topping; and Slapewath where the Way crosses the A171.

It is at Gribdale Gate that the Way crosses the line of the Cleveland Dyke, an igneous intrusion that is the only exception to the sedimentary nature of the rocks in the Park. It forms the eastern extension of a dyke that begins in the Island of Mull. Igneous rocks are those that have cooled from a molten state, the most well–known rock of the type being granite. It was about the time of the folding of the Jurassic sediments of the Park that lava intruded to form a nearly straight ridge running between Great Ayton and Newton–under–Roseberry, to fade out between Goathland and Ravenscar. Its course is often marked by frequently flooded excavations, since the rock was much used as a roadstone for local pony causeways.

Along the coast the retreat of the glaciers resulted in the deposition of much glacial drift, covering the earlier land-forms with a thick layer of boulder clay, sands and gravels. Where it filled old valleys the drift reached the coast and forms the cliffs at the heads of bays, as at Saltburn, Runswick, Whitby, Robin Hood's Bay and Filey. The pebbles of Robin Hood's Bay came from the erosion of the boulder clay; elsewhere, except between Ravenscar and Cloughton Wyke, the boulder clay can be seen on top of the pre–glacial sedimentary rocks of the cliffs. As inland, meltwater channels formed between the coastal hills and the North Sea ice, and these can be seen, especially along the coast south of Ravenscar. As the ice retreated, depositing drift, the streams, in settling down, often missed their pre–glacial courses which were blocked with the drift, and formed gorges in the rocks beneath the deposits.

The boulder clay appears flat along this part of the coast, for instance behind Robin Hood's Bay and many other places to the north. It is unclear whether this is due to a high sea–level or the forming of lakes towards the end of glacial times. On those level surfaces, parallel streams have often developed close together, producing ridges known as riggs between them, again as at Robin Hood's Bay, Whitby, Sandsend, Staithes and Saltburn.

From Saltburn to Filey the whole sequence of Jurassic rocks

found in the region is exposed as well as the covering of glacial deposits. Indeed the cliffs and bays display the rocks and formations well enough to have made the area popular with geologists.

Erosion is continually at work in the Park but is nowhere as well displayed as in the variations seen along the coast. The waves attack the bottom of the cliffs, especially during storms, undercutting them to form a wave–cut notch that eventually leads to a collapse. As this process is repeated a wave–cut platform can develop, such as the one to be seen at low tide in Robin Hood's Bay. This cliff erosion is apparent along the Way from Saltburn to Ravenscar, as is the constant erosion by streams and springs, but the rate of erosion is especially noticeable when man–made structures are endangered.

In general the shape of the coastline is due to the variety of rocks that make up the cliffs, and their resistance to erosion due to structure or hardness. North of Ravenscar the Liassic strata have created a coast where sandy bays occur between steep cliffs. The sandstones and ironstone tend to be harder than the shales that together make up the Lias, and just as the sandstones form ridges on the shore at Robin Hood's Bay, so they are responsible for the formation of North Cheek on its northern edge. Similarly Kettleness has formed because of the ironstone's resistance to erosion.

At Ravenscar itself, Old Peak has developed because of the famous Peak fault that has brought resistant rocks to the surface. The Ravenscar Geological Trail has been set up to point out the geological features of the area.

In contrast, to the south, there are fairly uniform, steep–cliffed coasts with pronounced terraces and boulder beaches that have developed because all the mid-Jurassic rocks have a similar resistance to erosion. A notable exception to this uniformity is Cloughton Wyke, which is on the Way.

South of Scarborough there is a similar uniformity, though here the Corallian limestones occur at the tops of the cliffs, above the Oxford clay, as the rocks of the Tabular Hills reach the coast. Again there is an exception, this time at Filey, where the Brigg is a finger of more resistant limestone brought to sea–level by a fault.

The higher Lias rocks have been worked since the Bronze Age
for jet, and have supported the mining industries that have
developed and declined in more recent times. From Osmotherley
around the escarpment of the Cleveland Hills and down much of
the coast, the Middle and Upper Lias outcrop and bear the marks
of economic exploitation. In crossing Scugdale, the rows of old jet
workings can be seen, marked by the waste tips that occur below
the mines in the jet rock. A small–scale jet industry still exists in
Whitby supplied with jet collected from the shore. The alum
shales yielded a complex compound used in tanning and dyeing
processes, and the extensive open mining evident on the
northern escarpment and on the coast has had the most
noticeable effect on the landscape of all the local industries. At
Carlton Bank are the remains of eighteenth–century alum
quarries with waste tips that show up pink, a characteristic of the
alum waste that is to be seen all along the Way. The quarrying
has been extensive enough to alter the shape of Slapewath and
several of the coastal cliffs. Even more intense, but nowadays less
noticeable, was the mining industry based on the ironstone of the
Middle and Upper Lias. It was founded at Grosmont, inland from
Whitby, after which the same seam was found to outcrop at
Skinningrove and along Cleveland Hills, particularly around
Guisborough. Roseberry Topping has had its shape altered by
mining for ironstone and alum.

The most recent industry to exploit the natural reserves of Park
is the extraction of potash, for agricultural use, from rocks of the
Permian period that exist at great depth. This mine is at Boulby.

Appendix II   Other Ways on the North York Moors

The Moors suffer more than most other upland areas from a plethora of named walks. The Lyke Wake Walk is the most famous of these, but such has been its usage (misusage ?) that the Park authorities now actively discourage walkers from following it.

Information on the Lyke Wake and the other moorland walks is available in several publications, and will not be duplicated here. One walk that is worthy of note, however, is the Missing Link.

It could be argued that the logical extension of the Cleveland Way, if one were sought, is the Wolds Way, another 'official' long–distance footpath; but many walkers appreciate a circular route that offers an easy solution to the problem of getting from finishing point back to starting point, especially if they have used their own transport. The Missing Link was devised by Malcolm Boyes in the mid-1970s to complete the circle of the North York Moors. It leaves the Cleveland Way at Crook Ness (028 934), going just north of west to Langdale Rigg End (929 948) and the fine walking across the Forestry Commission land around the Derwent Valley. The route then visits Levisham, from where it goes north–west through the Cropton Forest, crossing the top of Spaunton Moor to drop down to Hutton–le–Hole. From there the Link pathway goes north–west again, skirting Rudland Rigg and then going south from Birk Nab (626 912) to Helmsley.

The route is about 45 miles long; those who follow it lose the last section of the Cleveland Way to Filey, but gain some good viewpoints and fine dale walking.

Appendix III   Accommodation

There is a youth hostel at the start point of Helmsley — it is assumed that the Wayfarer will wish to travel with the prevailing wind at his back. On the coastal section the wind direction is in Neptune's hand and this section is well served by hostels:

Helmsley	— Carlton Lane, Helmsley	SE 616 840
Saltburn	— Riftswood Hall, Victoria Road, Saltburn-by-Sea	NZ 662 206
Whitby	— East Cliff, Whitby	NZ 902 111
Boggle Hall	— Boggle Hall, Mill Beck, Fyling Thorpe, Whitby	NZ 954 040
Scarborough	— The White House, Burniston Road, Scarborough	SE 026 907

Between Helmsley and Saltburn there are no hostels, a situation made no easier by there being long sections of walking away from civilisation.

Fly–camping on the Moors is not to be encouraged and will, in any case, be made awkward by lack of water. The Park authorities issue a list of accommodation on or close to the Way, including camping, and the best solution is to obtain this, and to make suitable arrangements beforehand. The list is obtainable from:

The North York Moors National Park Information Service,
The Old Vicarage,
Bondgate,
Helmsley,
North Yorkshire,
YO6 5BP

Tel No 0439–70657

Index